This book is vintage Richard Bewes ... direct, persuasive, encouraging, authoritative, full of interesting insights and amusing stories, but above all Biblically based and Christ centered at the same time.

After I started reading it, and with more than forty years experience of public speaking, I simply couldn't put it down. Not only that but I learnt many useful tips for the future.

It is immensely practical, covering nearly every aspect of public speaking, including such things as how to be well organised with sermon notes, illustrations and even criticism!

This book is in my judgement essential reading for any Christian speaker and an invaluable introduction for any potential speaker.

Lord Griffiths of Fforestfach
Goldman Sachs

Speaking in Public - Effectively should be required reading for Theological Colleges *everywhere* and for anyone called to preach or wishing to do so. It also has to be a most valuable aid for those who speak in public, irrespective of their subject. I travel a great deal and visit many churches. The majority of those speakers I have heard preach would benefit enormously by applying the contents of this book.

Richard Bewes is a wonderfully gifted speaker and writer. In this book we learn about his selfless attitudes and the methods he, himself, employs when speaking in public. This book is not theoretical - it is practical. It is easy to read, easy to understand and desperately needed.

David Suchet
Actor

All of us involved in public speaking will have had those occasions where we simply wanted to be taken in by a black hole after the sermon. The self-searching will normally have something to do with our preparation or simply the fact that we overlooked basic principles in our presentation of the material.

In this book, Richard Bewes takes the reader through important steps in preparing, presenting and progressing in public speaking. The fifteen chapters offer a wealth of invaluable principles and practical tips from one of Britain's best known and experienced preachers.

It will serve as a great foundation for those just starting out and a superb reminder for those of us who have been trying to get it right for rather more years.

Joel Edwards,
General Director, Evangelical Alliance, UK

SPEAKING IN PUBLIC EFFECTIVELY

RICHARD BEWES

CHRISTIAN FOCUS

ISBN 1-85792-400-2

First published in 1998,
Reprinted in 2002, 2005
by
Christian Focus Publications
Geanies House, Fearn, Ross-shire
IV20 1 TW, Great Britain

10 9 8 7 6 5 4 3 2 1

www.christianfocus.com

Cover design by Alister MacInnes

Printed and bound by
Nørhaven Paperback A/S, Denmark

Contents

Part Three: How To Progress

Foreword

This book is a must for every preacher, every Bible teacher and student, every mother with her little congregation about her in the home – every evangelist and missionary. In short, every Christian.

It sets the art of public speaking in a wonderful perspective.

My husband Billy Graham and I have heard Richard Bewes on both sides of the Atlantic I can hear his voice as it comes off the page. The illustrations and style make the text luminous – as if someone were holding a flashlight on the page.

It is a joy to recommend a book that is such a delight to read.

Ruth Bell Graham
Montreat, North Carolina

I dedicate this reprinted and revised edition of
SPEAKING IN PUBLIC - EFFECTIVELY
to Miranda Lewis, Pam Glover,
Kate Newman, Fiona Aldeburgh, Ian Roberts, Steven
Painter and numerous other colleagues at All Souls
Church.
It is they who ensure every week that the spoken word
gets recorded, edited and made available audio on-line
to our website

Richard Bewes, Spring 2002
www.allsouls.org

INTRODUCTION

It had been an amusing time in the Assembly, that day in Athens, twenty three centuries ago. An inexperienced orator had been insolent enough to test his skill in an arena normally reserved only for the best exponents of Greek rhetoric – and he'd been laughed off the platform.

Later on found the young Demosthenes moping dejectedly in the port area of the Peiraeus. An actor friend caught up with him: 'What's the trouble?'

Little by little it came out. The unrelenting cynicism of the audience. The flimsy content of the speech, the poor presentation. Demosthenes had stood crookedly: he'd lisped and stammered. He had persuaded nobody. His speaking career had utterly failed to take off.

'Ah, come on. Can't be that bad! I'm here to cheer you up. See if you don't become a great speaker!'

And that very thing happened. With encouragement and determination, the picture changed. Demosthenes took himself out of society for a while. He shaved only half his face, thus effectively keeping himself out of the social whirl of Athens. He left for the Aegean Sea.

There by the shore, the weak voice gained in strength as it was pitched against the roar of the breakers. Demosthenes would practise speaking with pebbles in his mouth, to improve his diction. He would declaim aloud while running uphill, to control his breathing. His utterances would be delivered in seclusion, with a sword suspended over his shoulder, to correct his ungainly stance. He studied the speeches of the great Thucydides, and wrote them out laboriously eight times.

He worked very hard.

The time came for another attempt in the daunting Assembly of Athens. This time it worked.

When Demosthenes' opponent had finished speaking, there was considerable applause. 'Marvellous oratory! Bravo!'

But as Demosthenes' speech came to a close, the entire audience was on its feet. His electrified listeners had been persuaded. 'Yes! We shall follow this man! We shall do as he says!' By dint of sheer hard work and sustained determination, Demosthenes had transformed himself into the greatest Greek orator of all – into a speaker whose words moved people to action.

And that, after all, is the difference between public speaking and an essay or lecture. When Demosthenes' exact contemporary, Aristotle, wrote his book on Rhetoric, he defined public speaking as *The Art of Persuasion*. That is the topic we shall address ourselves to in the pages of this book; perhaps with a single qualification. Although there will be plenty to encourage and equip speakers from many walks of life, I am writing primarily against the background of the theme that has dominated virtually a lifetime of speaking on my part – the Christian faith and the message of the Bible.

This book will meet readers at a variety of points. Some are speakers in the making. Some have yet to deliver their first talk. Some will be at college, training for a programme of speaking that will stretch for decades ahead! In all these cases, it is worth trying to get it *right* from the very start.

Some readers will be experienced speakers already. But, although this is not essentially a book about 'preaching' (for there exist plenty of good books on the subject), we who do preach never tire of sitting together and exchanging insights on this great romance of our lives - a calling that both inspires and frustrates, for no speaker worthy of the name is ever out of the learners' lane. There may, then, be something here for preachers too.

The art of persuasion. We shall attempt to do as Demosthenes did, and learn how to face people, how to put a talk together, how to think on our feet, how to move people to action! But a little less painfully, perhaps, than in the case of that ancient Greek.

RICHARD BEWES,
Written from All Souls Church, London W.1.
Revised January 2002

PART ONE

*****

HOW TO PREPARE

But set off gradually; the Lord will not despise the day of small things: pray heartily, that your spirit may be right with him, and then all the rest will be well.

It cannot be learned by industry and imitation only, as a man may learn to make a chair or a table: it comes from above; and if you patiently wait upon God, He will bestow this gift upon you, and increase it in you. It will grow by exercise.

John Newton
Letter to a prospective minister
July 25th, 1772

The Church was packed. I sat miserably on the platform while the service got underway. My time came. The pastor summoned me to the lectern and placed the microphone around my neck like a noose. The Bible shook in my hands and my knees felt weak.

'Oh God, help,' I prayed.

Stephen Lungu of Malawi,
Out of the Black Shadows, Monarch Books, 2001

I

GETTING STARTED

The speaker was wearing shorts, and his knees were visibly shaking as he addressed us at the summer houseparty. The voice was holding up well, but those knees! At any moment, I thought, they'll give way beneath him. I was taking in everything minutely, because I knew that it would be my turn the next morning – for the first time in my life!

Of course I would not have been due to speak at all had I not been nominated by the team leader.

'Let me do the games,' I had pleaded. 'Maybe I'll do the tennis coaching!'

Eventually I had caved in and agreed to give the required twelve-minute talk. That had been six weeks earlier; now the time had arrived, with twenty-four hours to go.

I was actually word-perfect. I had selected what I thought was an apt Bible sentence relating to my assigned subject of 'Christian Service', and work had begun on my preparation a full month ahead of time. I wrote and re-wrote, put in some stories to illustrate, and added what I hoped were relevant words of application. I had then committed the entire talk to memory, and reduced it to notes that would fit into my Bible. For ten days or so I had recited my talk to myself as I lay in bed. And of course I had prayed.

It was the knees that worried me now! The morning of my talk would probably be crisp, I reasoned. I was likely to feel the cold, and my fright would surely intensify the shivering. How could I stop myself from shaking like a jelly in front of those hundred people?

Eventually I hit on the idea of a bath, a really hot one, taken half an hour before the meeting. At the appointed time I emerged from the bathroom, relaxed and even a little limp, and took my place in the front row, ready to be summoned forward. My heart was pounding during the song that preceded the talk:

Come and serve the Master; he alone is true,

He will pardon sinners, therefore pardon you;

He has promised power, power to all who ask;

Power to conquer Satan, power for every task.

Up to the front; turn round and face the crowded room in my white tennis shorts, my breathing rather shallow, mouth dry, my Bible held tightly with both hands.

'Please sit down.'

The ice was broken. I opened the Bible. There were the notes, ready to prompt me. I began to disgorge the learnt words. My heart was still pounding, but my knees were steady! Help me to keep going, Lord. I'd started.

I never heard of anybody else who took a bath just before speaking. It was a habit I maintained for some years, until I began to feel less shaky. My mother was different; she always cleaned her teeth before speaking: 'Must have a clean mouth if you're going to speak for God,' she maintained.

I come, you see, from a family of speakers; both parents, my two brothers and my sister. The tradition seems to go back to a Tuesday night, September 26th, 1882, when my grandpa, Tommy, a boy of fourteen, responded to a mission address by the famed American preacher, D. L. Moody, then on a visit to Plymouth. Tommy was to become a preacher himself.

Years later my older brother Peter was preparing for his first talk.

'Don't go on too long!' he was warned.

'No, all right; I'll cut it down a little.'

A few more days passed.

Are you sure you won't exceed fifteen minutes?' he was asked, the day before the meeting.

'Um, well ... I hope not.' Dutifully he excised yet more material from his notes.

The talk, when it was given, lasted for three minutes flat.

The renowned Billy Graham, when aged eighteen, hardly believed he could speak at all. In tongue-tied admiration he accompanied his friend Grady Wilson to a meeting of twenty people at the 18th Street Mission in Charlotte, North Carolina. Grady elected to speak on a theme, *God's Four Questions*, borrowed out of a book. Billy thought to himself, 'How can my pal Grady keep going so fluently?' After speaking for half an hour, Grady paused: 'Now we come to God's second question!' (from *Just as I am*, Billy Graham: Harper Collins).

When Billy Graham did begin to get going, as often as not he would be practising his outlines to the rabbits in the early morning, or to the alligators in the cypress swamps – just to see if he could do it.

Public speaking – are people born or made for such a task? The question is immaterial once we can give the question a God-centred twist: *Is public speaking something that a person is called to?*

Once we can recognise this as the vital issue, then never mind whether you are a 'natural' or a 'made' speaker – you will dedicate yourself to the fulfilling of the call as you become aware that it has come to *you*. In no biblical case that I can recall was there ever a speaker for God and his people who was self-appointed. It was only the false prophets who set *themselves* up to speak in God's name:

> I did not send these prophets, yet they have run with their message; I did not speak to them, yet they have prophesied (Jer. 23:21).

How, then, in our present Christian era, can we discern a call from God to speak his word, let alone act upon it? It would, after all, be a terrible thing to stand up and speak a message for God if he has *not* summoned us to do so! Three guidelines will help.

Let the church recognise your speaking

It is right, of course that a flame is lit directly within the convictions of God's messenger. The Old Testament prophet Jeremiah was aware of an uncontainable fire burning inside himself (Jer. 20:9). In New Testament days the apostles Peter and John, faced by an official ban on their public speaking, replied, 'We cannot help speaking about what we have seen and heard' (Acts 4:20). Martyrs down the centuries, evangelists great and small, street preachers, Sunday School teachers and missionaries have all sensed a similar urge.

The morning after his dramatic conversion at the tent meeting he had intended to blow up with explosives, Stephen Lungu of Malawi was out, speaking on the buses! Although he now carried a Bible, he could neither read nor write; he was still sleeping under a bridge and eating out of trash cans. But for him it was the start of a lifetime of speaking; the flame had been lit.

Acknowledging all of this, we must recognise that it is to the church at large – *and to no other group on earth* – that the responsibility for declaring the message of God has been entrusted (Eph. 3:10). There must come a point, then, when every Christian who senses an inward urge to speak must come to terms with the church of Jesus Christ. Do the believers, who make up the church, recognise that this speaker has a call? If so, let *them* issue the invitation to speak, and provide a suitable format and platform.

Await your moment. Test your abilities separately, by all means, as Billy Graham did with his alligator addresses. Consult quietly with friends and advisors. But then leave it to others to take the initiative in getting you on your feet. Let God, through his people, *push* you into the arena, rather than push yourself forward. Let the church recognise your speaking, when it is ready to do so.

Let the church harness your speaking
You are not acting on your own account, but as part of a movement of witness called into being by Christ himself.

That is our context and framework as Christian public speakers. We are part of a larger outfit.

On occasions I have seen street orators at work in one or other of the world's cities. I may be handed a piece of literature at the same time. Inevitably I will turn to the back of the pamphlet with curiosity. Who does this speaker represent? Where is this message coming from? What are the credentials – or is the speaker self-appointed? It seems vital that God's messengers should be thoroughly accredited; in our case we must be in good standing with other Christians.

There is great protection when our speaking can be done within the partnership of the Christian fellowship and with its blessing. It means that we are standing with others, and they with us, in the great commission of Christ. But there is also power in such identification with the rest of the church, every time we open our mouth! It means that we can be sure of invaluable prayer support.

Years ago I was involved in a 'guest service' that was held in a church I used to lead at Harold Wood, in North-East London. I was the preacher for this special occasion of Christian outreach to friends and neighbours. Afterwards it emerged that the deputy headmaster of a nearby school, as a result of the service, had responded to the claim of Christ for the first time. But it was not my speaking that had particularly arrested his attention.

'It was your church treasurer,' he told me later. 'You got that man up at the front, half-way through the service, to tell us all how he had come to faith. He only spoke for five minutes. But in those five minutes I sensed something that I had never come across before. I could *feel* the whole congregation pulling for that man, unitedly. The experience completely bowled me over.'

Whether giving children's talks, speaking in the open air, leading campus Bible studies or addressing a sports meeting, the public speaker needs to have some recognisable corporate backing. One way or another, it should be the church that harnesses your speaking.

Let the church endorse your speaking

Who should benefit from your utterances? Ultimately the church! Your talks should so tie in to building up the life and health of the church, that it can be no other than a living tribute to your spirit of servanthood. Today there are too many speakers who consistently undermine and detract from the work of the churches. Worse, there are plenty of practitioners who are little better than self-serving spivs. They do not point their listeners in the direction of Christ and his people, but towards themselves and their own platform and interests. Frequently they have blown up some side-issue of Christian belief into a major tenet. They are described in the New Testament as 'blemishes' in the Christian fellowship, as 'shepherds who feed only themselves' (Jude 12).

By contrast, the apostle Paul writes in glowing terms of those he describes as 'partners' and 'fellow workers'. What they do, they do for the churches:

As for our brethren, they are messengers of the churches, the glory of Christ

(2 Cor. 8:23 RSV).

That is a wonderful description of speakers we can think of, on every continent, who have made it the business of their lives to support the faith and growth of churches everywhere. We love them. We love them for their hard work on our behalf, as they grapple with the message of the Scriptures and make it relevant. How glad we are when they come to our locality! We can live in the glow of their dedicated speaking for days.

Is it just possible that your speaking could actually be used to change a life? To unite a family? To transform the outlook of someone's workplace? Believe me, it happens. As I write this chapter, I think of a speaker, a relative unknown, working and studying in our own capital city of London. On delivering a single talk, on a controversial issue, in one of Britain's university cities, it was reported in the following week that his visit had altered the atmosphere of an entire college for the better.

These things begin – however small – with the God who calls and equips. We can believe that the scales are tilted in our favour. 'One word of truth outweighs the whole world,' wrote Alexander Solzhenitsyn; 'The truth is more powerful than tanks.'

'Give me,' said John Wesley, 'a hundred people who love God with all their hearts and fear nothing but sin, and I will move the world.'

Or to quote my own grandfather in some words that eventually found their way into my schoolboy's autograph album:

> I am only one,
> But I am one;
> I cannot do everything,

But I can do something.
What I can do,
I ought to do;
And what I ought to do,
By the grace of God I will do.

Why not make the great beginning as a speaker? But see to it that your fellow-believers are behind you and with you!

* * * * *

We must work for a world in which the gospels are as well known as Disney characters because, make no mistake about it, there is already a generation of English speakers for whom the Bible is a closed book. There is no time to lose.

The Rt. Rev. Richard Chartres,
Presidential address, London Diocesan Synod.
July 4th, 1996.

2

GETTING FOCUSED

The African Bible teacher was giving it his all, from a platform banked with flowers, at the Palais Du Centenaire. There we were, 8000 people, mostly young, met in Brussels for a *Bible event.*

That was the attraction, pure and simple; we were there to study the Bible together, drawn as we were from a score of countries.

'What if the River Nile had remained in Lake Victoria?' boomed the African, by way of illustration. 'If that had happened there would be no possibility of Egypt ever becoming a country!'

My American colleague on the platform nudged me.

'He's gone over time,' he whispered. 'Can you give him the red light?'

I was programme chairman. Theoretically I had the power to control our array of international speakers.

'I've given him two warning flashes already,' I murmured. Notwithstanding, I leant hard on the button that connected with the speakers' podium. But to no avail; by this time our Bible speaker was leaning on the red light with his hand, the other excitedly stabbing into the air as he made a fresh point.

The American was wriggling with anxiety. 'We've got to get everybody into their study groups right now!' he hissed.

I nodded.

'Leave it to me.'

The banks of flowers around the platform gave me excellent cover as I slid onto my stomach and crawled steadily across the platform until I reached the speaker. I tentatively grabbed an ankle and looked up.

'Stop!' I bleated.

The great man paused impressively. 'May God bless you all!' he beamed, and stepped back into his seat. Like a Jack-in-the-box I rose up in his place. 'Thank you very much indeed - let's do some follow-up now as we get into our study-groups!'

Eight thousand delegates dutifully got up. And every one of them carrying a Bible....

And that, in the very last analysis, was the magnet for those thousands of people - *the Bible*. Without the Scriptures to give a conference or youth event its main yardstick, you can invite all the speakers you want, but the inner appetite will never be satisfied and no lives will be changed. There are, today, any number of Christian organisations that put on extremely impressive programmes, but because the vital Bible emphasis has been edged to the side in favour of music, dramatic presentations and interviews with personalities, *their task becomes harder with every passing year.*

These alternative attractions can stimulate, but they cannot satisfy. Indeed the most superb oratory itself, if it lacks a substantial Bible content, can never carry a movement or church any great distance. It may attract a following for a period - but the policy is a short-term one

- it is only a matter of time; the gingerbread will eventually prove its inadequacy as a spiritual diet.

This happened in the case of the celebrated Scottish Presbyterian preacher of the nineteenth century, Edward Irving. In 1822 he was instituted as minister to a little-known London church with a congregation of about fifty. Within a year, hundreds were amassing to hear the flowing eloquence of London's latest sensation. The audience included the English statesmen George Canning and Robert Peel, the social reformers Jeremy Bentham and William Wilberforce, the poets Coleridge and Macauley, and the future Prime Minister William Gladstone – then a boy of fourteen.

The Duke of Sussex, the Earl of Aberdeen, Sir James Graham and the then Prime Minister Lord Liverpool were among Irving's frequent hearers. People had to be admitted by ticket, and hundreds were turned away.

But the crowds were being won by soaring oratory rather than through the secure Biblical anchorage of the speaker. As the novelty of Irving began to wane, slowly the numbers dissipated. Then, as the historian Thomas Carlyle (himself a friend of Irving) drily observed, 'There was now the impossibility to live neglected; to walk on the quiet paths, where alone it is well with us. Singularity must henceforth succeed singularity.'

This trait of 'singularity' took Irving, in his attempt to win back his audience, into the realms of millennialism, prophecy and the miraculous. Finally he was deposed from his church over his unbalanced views on the nature of Christ, and died in lonely disillusionment in his early forties (*Edward Irving and his Circle*, Andrew Drummond, James Clarke and Co).

It is the old principle of the angle; only get half a degree away from centre, and ten years down the line you will be way off course *and never know it*. From the start, the Christian who engages in speaking must do as the apostle Paul did, and get the focus in the right place:

> I did not come with eloquence or superior wisdom as I proclaimed to you the testimony about God. For I resolved to know nothing while I was with you except Jesus Christ and him crucified. I came to you in weakness and fear, and with much trembling. My message and my preaching were not with wise and persuasive words, but with a demonstration of the Spirit's power, so that your faith might not rest on men's wisdom, but on God's power
>
> (1 Cor. 2:1-5).

There, in a few crisp sentences, is our classic charter for a lifetime of speaking! It involves the firm rejection of unworthy and false approaches, in the Christian speaker's aim to stick to *God's* way. Those five New Testament verses contain recurring words that speak of stern, unbending resolve; *Not ... But ... Nothing ... Except*. I detect four clear facets of the task that faces us.

Our mandate: it concerns the testimony of God
Divine wisdom and human wisdom are seen in direct contrast. The apostle was emphatically *not* going to rely upon human insights and expertise, however brilliant or rhetorically acceptable they may have been. His mandate revolved specifically around 'the testimony about God'. This did not mean that he was unacquainted with the Greek thinking of his time. On the contrary, when he met with

the Epicurean and Stoic philosophers at Athens he knew how to quote their own poets to them (Acts 17:28). But it was the testimony and record of what God had done in Christ that he ultimately presented to his listeners.

From the beginning Paul was determined not to try to be clever or original, but simply to persuade his listeners to respond to what God had already made plain. That is our mandate too – despite the temptation to accommodate every trend of current thought.

A former London preacher Campbell Morgan once wrote, 'Our business is never to catch, but by eternal truth to *correct* the spirit of the age'.

It simply cannot be done without a firm and active belief in the Bible as the inspired Word of God. We must make up our minds that we are going to read the Bible for ourselves, on a daily believing basis – just as *Christians*, let alone as speakers.

The Bible is teeming with stories. It is a storehouse of divine promises. Its four mighty planks of *Creation, The Fall, Redemption* and *The Final Triumph* provide the reader with a raft built to last a lifetime; by it we shall be able to negotiate the dangerous shoals and rapids of modern thought.

Until and unless the Scriptures have begun to take a hold upon your own convictions, you certainly should not set out on the path of public speaking. Not as far as God's call is concerned! Naturally we shall never know the Old and New Testaments as well as we ought, but *a regular Bible intake should be our way of life from now on.*

I have sometimes heard it said that the regular 'Quiet Time' with the Scriptures is obsolete now, as a necessity for Christian effectiveness. I can only say that I would far prefer to hear a Bible talk from someone (however inexperienced) who regularly read the Bible, than from someone (however brilliant) who left it on the shelf. *What you do with the Bible on a daily basis is a statement of the value you place on it.*

So get up at the start of the day, with the Bible! More than that - take it into your day; carry it on your person, in your handbag or in your brief-case. If you cannot afford one the right size, put it on your birthday list. *We who speak for God should never be separated from his Book.*

In the dusty Tanzanian city of Dodoma, I met a public open-air speaker by the name of Zechariah Msonga, a giant of a man. Brought up as the son of a witch-doctor, he was later converted to Christ. He had never been to school, but with great determination he learnt to read, and plunged into the message from the Bible. He began to overflow with what he was learning. The harder passages he put to one side until his understanding could grow; but the stories of Jesus became the basis of his speaking. At first his Bible references tended to be taken out of context, and he would frequently lose track of the chronology. But the crowds who gathered to hear him in the market place were rivetted by this story-telling speaker with the glowing face and open Bible. The Scriptures had provided him with a bottomless resource. Hundreds upon hundreds found God as they listened to Zechariah. He had been given a mandate and he knew it. It concerned the testimony of God. Here is a second facet of 1 Corinthians 2:1-5.

Our Message: it centres in the Cross of Christ

Paul was resolved to know nothing 'except Jesus Christ and him crucified' (v.2). We should not infer from this that the great apostle was speaking directly about the death of Jesus every time he stood up. But everything he said and wrote was coloured by this central Christian truth.

When he dwelt at length upon human sinfulness, it was in order that the wonder of the Cross and its forgiveness could be highlighted. When he spoke about the church, none of his hearers would have been in doubt about its indebtedness to its once-crucified Head. If the Holy Spirit was the subject of a particular message, it was to get across the point that the Spirit had come to make personal *in* them, all that Christ by his death had accomplished *for* them.

When Jesus, risen from the grave, accompanied the two downcast disciples on the Emmaus Road the first Easter Sunday evening, he began to rebuild their shattered world-view by saying, 'Did not the Christ have to suffer these things and then enter his glory?' (Luke 24:26). The rest of the journey he spent in explaining to them how 'all of the Scriptures' related and led up to his saving Messiahship; the Fall, the giving of the law, the Passover, the Covenant with Israel, the Levitical sacrifices, the failed monarchy, the message of the prophets, the Exile – *everything*.

Let any faithful representative of Christ get up to speak – and the Cross will never be very far away. To forget this would be equivalent to writing a book on Marconi without any reference to radio, or making a documentary on the Wright brothers and editing out the section on flying. The death of Jesus was unlike any other death in the history of the world. In the words of Augustine, sixteen hundred years ago, 'What a death, that gave death its death-blow.'

Now we who speak for God must hold to this central emphasis on the Cross. Once we imagine that the power of the Cross is incomplete without the addition of some other ingredient to the message ... and there will be a loss of power. Then comes the attempt, born of desperation, to find an alternative source of power – and within a comparatively short space of time that 'supplementary' emphasis will take over centre stage. Enthusiasm may reign for a period; great claims may be made, but the 'power' will be human-based, incapable of truly changing people, let alone of denting society.

> Jews demand miraculous signs and Greeks look for wisdom, but we preach Christ crucified; a stumbling-block to Jews and foolishness to Gentiles, but to those whom God has called, both Jews and Greeks, Christ the power of God and the wisdom of God
>
> (1 Cor. 1:22-24).

The hymns that Christians choose to sing are a dead give-away as to where their epicentre is. If the Cross has any kind of hold upon our lives, we will sing and speak about it, as has happened in all true Christian stirrings through history. Our message centres in the Cross of Christ. But there is more.

Our method: it commits us to the power of the Spirit

John Wesley's speaking transformed English society two and a half centuries ago. 'God worketh in you,' he once observed, 'therefore you can work; otherwise it would be impossible.' Wesley was referring to the Holy

Spirit, universally promised to every believer in Christ from the day of Pentecost onwards:

> You will receive power when the Holy Spirit comes on you, and you will be my witnesses ....
>
> (Acts 1:8).

The Holy Spirit is simply the unseen presence of Christ within the lives of his followers. It is he (for the Holy Spirit is a person) who is the secret behind every work of effective Christian outreach, and every public utterance that has inspired the lives of people. No one should step forward as a Christian speaker who has not begun to know, in the power of prayer, what it is to be filled with the Holy Spirit, as a regular, continuing and daily experience. Without this filling, our talks may be beautifully constructed, witty and entertaining, and may evoke plenty of adulation ... but the power of God to change lives permanently will be missing. No wonder the apostle Paul was so insistent, in his repeated use of the words *not* and *but*:

> My message and my preaching were *not* with wise and persuasive words, *but* with a demonstration of the Spirit's power, so that your faith might *not* rest on men's wisdom, *but* on God's power
>
> (1 Cor. 2:4, 5).

It is not that the speaker for God is necessarily *conscious* of the Spirit's power flowing through the words; it is more likely that there will be an awareness of personal inadequacy, of the 'weakness', 'fear' and 'much trembling' of Paul's experience.

Joe Church was such a speaker, years ago. God used this English medical doctor to kindle a great spiritual revival in the church of East Africa, a mighty tide of the Spirit that touched the lives of hundreds of thousands. I remember him coming to address a student gathering in my college days.

'There's a special speaker coming tomorrow; Joe Church.'

'Isn't he the revival man?'

'That's the one; a guy filled with the Holy Spirit.'

'Wow.'

But when the talk was given, I couldn't, for the life of me, see where the magic lay. There were no antics, no purple passages. It was all rather, well ... *ordinary*. Yet God had chosen to use this individual to touch countless people, by the power of his Spirit.

To be filled with the Holy Spirit requires, *first*, that we remove the blockages to his filling. He is, after all, the *Holy* Spirit. Daily repentance for known sins and a refusal to lie down in the battle for Christlike living provide the key. *Second*, we are to open our lives in obedience to the lordship of Jesus Christ, as we read the Scriptures and submit to him in daily prayer. *Third*, we are to share the wonderful things of the Christian life with others. Paradoxically, the way to be filled is to be *emptied*!

You can prove this yourself. You can take on a challenging piece of service as a Christian, and you will make the amazing discovery that *in the performance of your task* you are being filled and fulfilled. When it is all over, as likely as not you will feel *better* than before you began. This is related to the filling of the Spirit. Try it out!

This has nothing to do with speaking in an abnormal tone of voice or adopting holy mannerisms. The Spirit-filled person is not *self*-conscious at all. So it was in the days of the New Testament – where there is no record of an individual declaring 'I have been filled with the Spirit'. It was left to other people to draw that conclusion. The answer to the question 'Are you a Spirit-filled person?' should probably be 'You'd better ask my family! Ask someone who knows me'.

But ask to be filled, every day – whatever the task. Apply this to everything you touch. When it comes to public speaking, there are plenty of practical lessons to be shared, and we will go on to consider them in future chapters of this book. But one thing is indispensable, as far as 'method' is concerned. Christian speaking commits us to the power of the Spirit. And last of all? Here is a fourth requirement of the 'focused' public speaker:

Our ministry: it calls for the changing of lives
I have referred to this a number of times already. There is an approach to public speaking that can obscure the meaning, and empty the Cross of its power, even though the Scriptures are being appealed to. It happens when the speaker forgets that *this is a life-changing word and it has already changed me.*

The public speaker is not up there at the front simply to impart information. If it were just that, then our business would be that of *lecturing*. But this is most definitely not a lecture! Naturally the lecture occupies an honourable place in public life. It is a recognised form of communication. But ...!

The fact is, if you are on the threshold of a speaking career, *you have not got long to work it out before your course is set*. Speaking in order to persuade, lecturing in order to inform, or entertaining in order to attract? Just to name but three possible alternatives! It is true that every good talk will be delivered in order to inform – but the object is not merely the gathering of information. It is equally true that the talk will fail if it does not engage the attention of the listeners – so attention must be given to our presentation. But we are not there primarily to amuse.

This is what kept the apostle Paul on track, as he firmly set aside the accepted rhetorical forms of his day. That meant a certain limitation in his approach. If, at the end of the day, the listeners can only remember the form and style of the speaker – either the boring monologue on the one hand, or the jokes and laughs on the other – then the form has taken over from the content, and we have failed.

Don't be content to adopt the various 'artforms' that much of public speaking has lapsed into today. Don't become a clone of other speakers – however much you may admire them. If God has called you, he will shape you in a way that is uniquely and wonderfully *yourself*. Ask him for his help as you get focused for this greatest of privileges.

* * * * *

Even an apostle must read. He is inspired and yet
he wants books! He had seen the Lord, and yet he
wants books! He had been caught up into the Third
Heaven, and yet he wants books!

C.H. Spurgeon on the apostle Paul.
From a sermon on 2 Timothy 4:12.

3

GETTING ORGANISED

Standing up to deliver a talk is even more of an excitement and a challenge than acting in a play. The actor in a play comes on, line perfect, after a succession of painstaking rehearsals. The props are organised; there is even a prompter within whispering distance.

Not so for you, the public speaker! *The expectation is that you will get the whole thing right at the first attempt and with no chance of a re-run.* Hence the need of a few props yourself, indeed of every ounce of encouragement and resource that you can scrape together.

What are these props?

Begin with the Bible. The Bible's view of itself is that it, being the word of God, has the capacity to change people's whole lives. A single sentence can do it.

I was encouraging friends at church one day to learn a verse of the Bible by heart. We did it together, out loud. 'The reference first,' I announced. 'Then the words. And then the reference again! Ready?' And off we went:

Ephesians 2: 8, 9 - For it is by grace you have been saved, through faith - and this not from yourselves, it is the gift of God - not by works, so that no-one can boast.

It's too much like going back to school thought Pauline, a young married woman who was present. However she participated in the exercise and thought no more about it.

The next day one of her friends stopped her.

'I've been watching you over these months, Pauline. I know you are a Church person, and you've got something I want to have! Can we talk?'

'Of course,' said Pauline. 'Come round to my place any time.'

'*I mean now*!'

Pauline felt trapped, unready. She didn't know what to say or do. How could she explain the Christian way of salvation? Why, she didn't know a single verse of the Bi ... *yes she did*. She'd learnt it the night before! Hesitantly she repeated Ephesians 2:8, 9, explaining to the best of her ability the meaning of God's free gift. Later that day her friend was to make the great decision to follow Christ. And all on the strength of a single Scripture verse.

If it can happen in a one-to-one exchange, we can believe that the miracle can be repeated - and multiplied - in the special dynamic of a speaker addressing a group. It is a matter of *confidence in the Bible*, and a lifetime commitment to the understanding of its message.

As people of the Word, then, we shall be into the fascinating world of *books*. Books to help in the background and the understanding of the Scriptures. Books to help in the development of a biblical framework of thinking for the whole of life. Where are you going to find these books for the steady building up of your Christian library?

In the section marked 'Religion', perhaps in your local bookstore? I'm afraid not! Here in the West, they'll be into novel 'startling' theories of a Jesus far removed from the Christ that we have come to know and love in the Bible. Those authors come broadly under the category of deviationists denounced by the apostle Paul as those who 'peddle the word of God for profit' (2 Cor. 2:17). No lives will be led to a knowledge of God by these sensation-mongers; they have not earned the respect of international Bible scholars.

Do we go, then, to specifically Christian bookshops for the basis of our reading and study? Answer; yes ... but be choosey! A myriad of titles will face you in most Christian bookshops, many of them right on target as far as Bible understanding is concerned, some of them with only echoes of the Bible, and quite a few actually off course. Beware the principle of the widening angle!

Let older Christians in your own fellowship give help and advice at this point. Read the reviews in the Christian press, and begin to know your reviewers. Develop a healthy scepticism towards books that purport to be 'biblical'. After all, have you ever seen a book from a deviationist movement or sect that advertises itself on the cover as *unbiblical*? Of course not; they all purport to be communicating the unvarnished truth!

Begin modestly, and let your library develop its own balance. You will be acquiring *Bible commentaries*, by authors with a reverent attitude to Scripture. In addition you will be on the look-out for books that present the

Old and New Testament background. There will be *reference books*, expensive enough to put on your birthday list, - including illustrated Bible dictionaries with information on virtually every Bible topic going, Bible atlases, and concordances that give the reference for every word that features in Scripture. It was my Aunt Pearl who gave me my Young's Analytical Concordance for my twenty-first birthday, and a fabulous gift it was. Today there are computerised concordances and Bible helps available for those with the equipment to use them.

What else? *Doctrinal books* must figure high, helping aspiring speakers to grapple with the great fundamental teachings of our faith; God, the person of Jesus Christ, the Holy Spirit, the Cross, salvation, the Church, Eschatology and the end of the age. Look out for trusted authors who have wrestled with topics of *Controversy and modern thought*. They are the writers who show us where the great landmarks are in contemporary thinking, and how the strongholds of error are to be overthrown. John Stott, J.I. Packer, Don Carson, Lesslie Newbigin, Billy and Ruth Graham, Francis Schaeffer, Os Guinness, Joni Eareckson Tada, David Wells, Anne Graham Lotz, Alec Motyer - these are among the many authors I personally have valued in recent years.

And don't forget the area of *Christian history and mission*. Some of the great spiritual movements and leaders of the past lie hidden in unopened pages, only waiting their turn to thrill or challenge a new generation. What do people know of the martyr Polycarp; of the heroic battle for truth by Athanasius, or the first 'Bible smuggler' William Tyndale? What of the past proclaimers of Christ - Luther, Knox, Whitefield, Jonathan Edwards, Finney and

Moody? Have you ever heard of *the Maréchale* Kate Booth? Or of Gladys Aylward, the diminutive parlour maid who was called to China?

Speakers who have missed out on the sheer adventure of Christian history often give the impression that nothing has happened over the last 2,000 years! Never mind how slowly it comes together; see to it that your knowledge of the past provides your speaking with a reservoir of ever-increasing depth.

There are evangelistic books, devotional books, books on ethics, mission and topical issues – and we have not begun to mention the avalanche of information alongside of the Christian faith and the Bible! Did you know that President Harry Truman had read some 3,000 books by the time he was fourteen? You and I may not equal his intake, but it is a balanced and comprehensive reading that assists the public speaker to present a rounded-off and credible world-view to any audience – *whatever the topic*.

But let's move on – to the fascinating subject of *your system for speaker's notes, illustrations and general indexing*.

'Philip, I want you to tell me exactly how you organise yourself as a speaker. How do you write your notes? Where do you store them and how can you find them again?'

It was a young people's summer camp, and I was an assistant leader for the first time. I made my choice of an advisor carefully; Philip Tomson was one of the senior leaders, and I'd marked him down as someone who had it all worked out long ago.

'My system is quite simple Richard. Come and have a look.'

Philip Tomson is dead now. But I shall feel indebted to him always, for helping me to begin a system that has served me since my early twenties.

We were not into computers and word-processors in those heady little days at camp! I will touch on such developments later. But first, let me describe my system, a system that I have not been able to improve upon ever since I started speaking.

The notes themselves! Really, they ought not to be too *big*. All too often I have listened to speakers whose notes seem to dominate, even to distract from, the message they are giving ... because the impression given is of large, white turning *pages*. Subconsciously, I find myself counting, *that's the fifth page; wonder how many more to go?* And each one covered with detailed type.

It's fair enough if you are speaking in the Melbourne Cricket Ground, or at Madison Square Garden, from a podium the size of a four-poster bed! But most of us will not be doing that. The notes should not intrude.

Then, as a regular rule, the notes should not be too *small*. Supposing you arrive to give your talk in a badly-lit room, or where the glare from the windows is right in your eyes, or where a spotlight is trained onto your face?

Very early on I took Philip Tomson's advice and decided, as a broad principle, that I would opt for notes that were 6 x 4 inches, that is 152 x 102 millimetres. The advantage of this size is that – at least in the United Kingdom – this is a standard size for *card indexes* ... and here lay my second decision – as to how and where to *store* my notes.

For I had decided from the start that, when the talk was over, I would not discard the notes – at least not immediately. If I had spent a number of hours on my material, it somehow seemed a waste to jettison the fruits of those studies, the moment the talk had been delivered. So I use 6 x 4 inches steel card index cabinets, 15 inches deep. I keep them on a table about 24 inches deep, so that as I pull out the cabinet interiors, they don't overbalance onto the floor.

The talks were to be stored in two categories – by *books of the Bible*, from Genesis to Revelation, separated by labelled card index tabs; and by *topics*, tabulated from A to Z.

I do recommend cards, not paper! Paper becomes dog-eared, creased and torn very easily, and does not take kindly to a card index. To illustrate, I have just pulled out one of my first talks ever – on Amos chapter 6. It has seven cards, all in good condition. Along the right hand edge of the first card I had written 'CCB' (Christ Church Beckenham), then the date and time; next 'Amos 6: A realist from the Desert ... 22 minutes'. Then I had coloured the right hand edges of all seven cards in blue for easy distinguishing from the differently-coloured cards of other talks that would eventually find their way into the 'Amos' section.

In this way the occasion, book and title of the address are all facing upwards as the card goes into the cabinet; one of many small future time-savers.

I can't pretend that I would give the identical talk again now. As Bible knowledge and experience have grown, I find I need to go through my card index once a year and weed out those talks that I would never even *refer* to again. But in fact, Amos 6 is still there, saying *'Use part of me if you need to*!'

Astonishingly, I still possess and use the small ring-binder notebook I bought when I first started speaking. It takes 6 x 4 inch cards, is black, slim and compact, and can be slipped into an inside pocket. It is, therefore, extremely handy. When the binding began to wear out, a church member kindly re-bound it in leather, so ensuring that it will see me out!

A correctly-sized device for punching holes into the cards standardises them for insertion into the ring-binder, and keeps them together and in the right order. This is important – I have seen disaster strike on more than one occasion when loose notes have either fluttered away or have got in the wrong sequence in the shuffling fingers of an over-nervous speaker.

I cover both sides with my notes, for the sake of conciseness, and also to reduce by half the number of cards that need to be flipped over. As a matter of fact it is unnecessary – and distracting for the listeners – for notes to be 'flipped' in an overt way. There are ways of handling notes that don't divert the attention.

And what of those elusive *illustrations*, snippets from newspapers and vivid quotations culled from our regular reading? It is the illustrative material that so often 'lifts' a talk, giving it a breath of fresh air, a ray of sunlight, a flash of humour. Jesus did this, and so can we. Unless we are very unusual beings, we shall simply not be able to remember the great majority of incidents, sayings and illustrations that are coming at us all day long.

From the very beginning of my speaking, I began another card index, for cards of a smaller format, a standardised 5 x 3 inches, or 128 x 76 millimetres. In my daily diary would be clipped a few blank cards, useful for memos, but also for the recording of illustrations *as they came to me*. It is uncanny; leave that illuminating 'idea' ungarnered, for even ten minutes ... and it's gone. Ideas, episodes and quotations from my reading – the aim was to get them immediately onto a card, which could then be placed in the 5 x 3 inches index, grouped alphabetically under the most obvious truth that it seemed to illustrate. 'The Fall', 'Fame,', the 'Family', 'Fasting' – here are just a few from the 'F' section.

I now have thousands of these illustrations at hand. With the appropriate holes punched in them, they can, if necessary, be clipped into the ring binder with the main notes for a talk if, for example, a quotation proves somewhat laborious to copy out.

Storage and retrieval; an obvious approach for many modern speakers is by way of the computer, more specifically – for those who can afford it – the electronic organiser. More expensive, of course, than the time-honoured card index, it nevertheless offers certain significant advantages. If, for example, you want to find that 'untraceable' stored quotation, you only have to tap in a single key word from the quotation or its source, and the screen will bring it up. Talks, illustrations and sources can all be typed, stored, accessed and printed out with the help of an electronic organiser with word-processing facility and a printer. It can be done in the back of a car, and the notes can, if desired, be printed onto standardised cards ready for eventual storage.

Today there is software available to help speakers and preachers with their illustrations and stories, and – while such speakers' discs must be used with restraint and caution, as we shall see in chapter 5 – they may nevertheless provide an initial pool of ideas for the inexperienced.

Even the best 'system' is no guarantee of an effective talk. The world still remembers when President Ronald Reagan's autocue broke down on him; or when a speaker on BBC's prestigious *Thought for the Day* completed page one of his manuscript, live on air, only to discover that page two had magically disappeared!

I still go cold on remembering an occasion when, half-way to Germany for a speaking series, I realised that all my notes were in a pile on my study floor back in London.

You can be superbly organised and have all the back-up systems in the world, *but the best back-up that any speaker can have is to **know the talk***; *to be captivated by the topic*!

Someone reading this chapter has a lifetime of speaking ahead ... you are going to be giving hundreds and hundreds of talks. How is a talk put together? How does it take shape? We'll keep that for the next chapter.

* * * * *

Night after night here in this Garden I intend to be only a messenger to give God's message to the people of New York. My messages each evening will be based on the Bible which I believe to be the inspired Word of God. I am not here to give you my thoughts – but God's thoughts.

May 15th 1957, from Billy Graham's first sermon in sixteen weeks of preaching at Madison Square Gardens.

4

THE ANATOMY OF A TALK

Years ago at college, one of the duties assigned to me in the Christian fellowship was that of taking careful notes on the weekly evangelistic address given by an invited speaker. The idea was that I should then send a summary of the talk to the next speaker on the list. In this way it was hoped that some degree of continuity could be ensured throughout the programme.

The habit of note-taking taught me a lot; how speakers began and ended, whether they strayed away from the topic or Bible passage they had been given, how their main points fitted together, and how stories, humour and sayings of the famous could be successfully harnessed.

I soon learnt that no talk is really like another. Some of our speakers had three main points to make; some were four, five or even six-pointer speakers, while other addresses resembled an impressionistic painting, with layers of colour and vivid imagery being generously applied in all directions.

Despite the variety, however, I noted the fact that the best speakers – no matter how many their points – invariably held to *a single, overriding theme that dominated everything they said.* Apart from that vital quality, it seemed that there was no 'approved' format.

The late Festo Kivengere, a marvellous Ugandan speaker, used to be invited all over the world. Yet he would compare himself unfavourably to others, with a disarming humility.

'Take your John Stott!' he once confided to me. 'He would put me to shame. I would listen to him in the morning conference, all neat and clear. I would scratch my little head and come on to speak in the afternoon, with my little bits and pieces hanging out all over!'

Yet there was no doubting that these two great speakers admired and learnt from each other.

We must be careful, then, when establishing the ground rules of speaking, not to restrict ourselves to a strait jacket that is unnatural to the culture or personality we have been bequeathed. But, bearing in mind these cautions, there is such a thing as a recognisable 'anatomy' of a talk. At the very least it must have a beginning, a middle and an end. In this it bears comparison with any piece of verbal communication. Years ago there was a British radio producer, whose advice on the 'shape' of a programme is still a byword with many broadcasters. His name was Brian Mickey.

'Start bright!' he would urge. 'Then go brighter. Thirdly, slow it down – and finally, go out with a bang!'

Basic to his maxim was the necessity of *movement and shape* in all of our communication.

What is the aim of the Christian speaker? The Bible gives us a magnificent definition:

The Anatomy of a Talk

They read from the Book of the Law of God, making it clear and giving the meaning so that the people could understand what was being read

(Neh. 8:8).

That is exactly it. We are not up there on our feet in order to speak for ourselves. We are there for God and his Word; the privilege is enormous, the responsibility is frightening. Start with the 'easy' passages; that way there is less chance of causing damage! Be a student of the Scriptures; transfer the findings of your study into a notebook. Get a wide-margin Bible, and insert at the side of a text or passage helpful 'outlines' that have come to you. One day they may be used to help others. I have done this since I was a student, and the benefits have been cumulative over the years.

The anatomy of a talk – let's stay with the organic metaphor, as we think about the construction of a talk.

Give it a head

For myself, the only way to begin the direct preparation is to start writing! The Bible is there, open in front of me. I then get a large piece of paper, and at the top write out the topic and the Bible reference. Then I draw a line down the length of the page, somewhat to the right of centre. The wider, left hand section is reserved for my jottings on the *meaning* of the text or passage; the right is given over to stories and such illustrative material as may occur to me during my preparation.

I pray for understanding and I read – and re-read – from the Bible. I am trying to isolate the *one* dominant thought conveyed by the passage. What is it? Bible commentaries can often help at this point, notably in recent years *The Bible Speaks Today* series, published by Inter-Varsity Press.

I am trying to find the right direction for this talk, in a way that is true to the Scriptures; to set the tone in my introduction, to give the talk a head! As I gaze at the Bible's words I try to follow a three-fold guideline, remembered over many years, from John Stott. With the help of the Holy Spirit we are to establish:

The *original* meaning
The *natural* meaning
The *general* meaning

What did these words mean to the *first* readers? How do the words *naturally* read – in a way that hasn't been manipulated or twisted? And does my understanding of what the sentence is saying tie in with the surrounding context and with the rest of the Bible in *general*? For the Bible – though often confronting us with paradox and mystery – will never contradict itself.

Determine that God's Word will shape your talk; resist the temptation to pour the Bible into *your* mould. There are too many one-theme-only speakers – they become known for the fact that, whatever the passage, they are scratching away at their particular pet subject. To parody an eighteenth century hymn:

Ten thousand thousand are their texts,
But all their sermons one.

Two centuries ago, Charles Simeon, who ministered in Cambridge for fifty momentous years, once observed,

'My endeavour is to bring out of Scripture what is there, not to thrust in what I think might be there.'

This is the hardest part of the preparation, understanding the elusive 'one thing' that God is saying in this passage, and will be saying through your talk in a few days' time! At times you will become desperate in your inability to see the passage straight, and you will find yourself on your knees, Bible and pad in front of you, praying, pleading, scanning; then taking a break to clear your head.

There is no set pattern to this. Sometimes the light can break through in ten minutes! More usually it will be an hour, perhaps several hours. *The taking of a break is wise.* You may think that you've grasped the main point, only to come back a day later to discover that you hadn't got it at all.

But at some point the mists clear. The paper is filled with scribbles. Whispers of how the truth can be introduced and then illustrated are beginning to edge on to the screen of your mind. Even an opening may be suggesting itself. I must admit, I have heard a few unfortunate beginnings over the years:

'The subject is beauty.'
'This is the stuff of which fairy tales are made.'
'My subject this morning is, *What is Wrong with the World*?'
'Have you heard this one?'

On the majority of occasions, the wisest start is that which begins with the reading out of the text or a part of the Bible passage that is yours to speak on. This has two great advantages; first from the outset, it amounts to a declaration of your authority; you are not here primarily to give your own opinions, you are speaking from *God's* Book. The second advantage, for the inexperienced, is that such an exercise enables you to get used to the sound of your own voice while you are reading directly from the page. If your listeners also are equipped with Bibles, then all eyes will be reassuringly *down* at that point, and not on you!

Speakers should not grudge the spending of the greater part of their preparation on the start of the talk. A good beginning promises well for the rest of the talk. At least it has got a head.

Give it some bones

Most of us who speak tend to overestimate the capacity of our listeners to retain the substance of what we are saying. A second discipline, then, is to ask ourselves: Does this one great truth you are putting across break down naturally into digestible chunks? Do these subsidiary points all relate to the dominant theme? Will they crystallise for the hearers what the passage or text was saying? Are they simple enough and memorable enough to remind people at a later date of what they received from your talk?

I try, as far as possible, to *avoid* headings such as:

1. The nature of the prayer.
2. The basis of the prayer.
3. The purpose of the prayer.
4. The content of the prayer.

Those headings are only useful in providing the speaker with some natural breaks. *But they have not got truth built into them*. We have to realise, I am afraid, that quite a lot of our listeners will be doing very well if they manage to retain even the headings of the talks that they hear. It is, then, worth while ensuring that those headings will be as memorable as possible. Memorable, not because they comprise a clever outline, but rather because they *sum up* clearly and vividly what God is actually saying in his revelation.

As I write this chapter, we have been following the book of Daniel in our Sunday preaching. My most recent assignment was chapter 8 – 'Kingdoms that cannot last'. It was a difficult passage, but I tried to anchor the teaching with these three headings, as I described the nature of kingdoms that are outside the rule of God. They are, I declared:

1. Saturated with success.
2. Inflated with power.
3. Destined for failure.

One of the tests is to see if you can remember your own headings, forty-eight hours after speaking!

Whether it is a single text of Scripture, a passage or a topic, it is worth working hard on the framework of the talk – to give it some bones.

Give it some flesh

At this stage in my preparation, I am usually onto a second piece of paper, with my introduction mapped out and my headings in place. By now the talk ought to have got a grip of me. I am not dominating it; it is dominating me! As one of our trainee speakers at our church of All Souls told me after delivering a talk, 'For days it completely consumed me'.

In a very real sense, the hardest part is *done*; that of the working out of Theme, Aim and Structure. But now the skeleton needs some body. Body – not padding! Quite a lot of modern speaking follows this pattern: Joke, a second joke; *Introduction* (too long); *first heading*, joke, story; *second heading*, joke, quote, joke; *third heading*, step up tempo, dramatic story; *long, sloppy ending*.

Is that what God wanted? Come back to your calling as you work out the talk's *matter*. Ask God the Holy Spirit to help you as once again you scan the Scripture passage before you. What have you missed? What was that gem in the commentary that caught your attention an hour ago? Find it – ah, there it is! It fits in well with your second point, or does it? No, the third point! Help me, Lord, to build around that bit. I love it – may my listeners love it too.

Little by little it is building up. But can I see where and how the talk will *end*? I must start to *anticipate* the conclusion within the main body of what I am saying. Can't have an ending that is just tagged on! The whole talk must hold together if it is to make that one stabbing point.

I am still at the scribbling stage. There's more to put into this talk. Yes, it's getting some body by now. But it needs more:

Give it wings

It's 'the wings' that make a twenty-minute address feel like only five minutes! By contrast, it is the absence of those personal and imaginative touches than can sometimes leave a talk with a feeling of woodenness, with the listeners glancing tiredly at their watches after only a few minutes in. This is where the jottings on the right hand side of my preparation page begin to edge their way into the body of the talk; that marvellous quotation from a sports journal, the moving story from Cambodia, the amusing incident on the subway. There will be more on this topic in the next chapter; for the present, let us establish that there is an element in every good talk that helps it to 'take off', and arrest the listeners with a truth that they will remember forever!

Way back on September 1st, 1957, Billy Graham spoke to some 120,000 people crammed into New York's Times Square. Basing his address on the visit of the apostle Paul to Mars Hill in Athens, his text was Acts 17:23:

> For as I passed by, and beheld your devotions, I found an altar with the inscription *to the unknown God*.

The speaker might have made four academic points. Instead he emulated Paul – drawing attention, not to surrounding religious altars, as in the case of Mars Hill, but to their modern equivalent in Times Square; the surrounding advertising hoardings for four cinema films then showing. One was Cecil B. de Mille's *The Ten Commandments*. Another was a picture called *The Lonely Man*. A third was entitled *The Walking Dead*, and to round off a talk that lived forever in the minds of the listeners, was *Love in the Afternoon*.

Preaching the Christian message through movie titles!

You and I might have missed them – it took an imaginative mind to spot the four hoardings that would give wings to a talk that was to change many lives.

At a certain point you are asking yourself, *Is this talk going to fly?* When that point is reached, you can begin actually to write out the talk. Write, or type - I've done both, using the standardised cards that I've become familiar with over several decades. Writing out your own cards is an excellent discipline; it helps you to think on paper. And people who have learnt to think on paper will eventually discover that they have developed the ability to think on their feet. Writing out the talk assists you in the carving out of the right word, and therefore in the stretching of your vocabulary. You will find one day that you are able, seemingly, to pull words out of the air on those occasions when notes are inappropriate.

As I write the talk, I am trying to 'see' the audience. Who are these people? Are they old or young? Many or few? Are they a cultural mix? What kind of auditorium will I be speaking in? In the week this chapter is written, I am due to preach at St. Paul's Cathedral, London. I must watch it, then; can't be too intimate; the pulpit there is almost a building in itself ... and beware of the four-second echo! Cut *down* the material then; keep it tight.

Write it like you're talking. If I was speaking to one individual about this great truth, how would I say it? Now write that sentence down. Keep it moving. Keep it simple; avoid the all-Bible paperchase. Make the sentences crisp and short, and don't feel obliged to cram in all that you know about your topic or passage. Stick to the main point!

A former attorney-general, Sir James Scarlett, became famous in England during the nineteenth century for his great success as an advocate. When he was asked for his secret, he explained it by saying that *the one great point* of the case had to be pressed home, without overmuch dwelling on secondary issues, and keeping it short enough for his main case to stick:

> I find that when I exceed half an hour I am always doing mischief to my client; if I drive into the heads of the jury unimportant matter, I drive *out* matter *more important* which I had previously lodged there.

A black speaker once put it: 'First I tell them what I'm going to tell them. Then I tell them. Then I tell them what I told them.'

And even then, are they going to retain it all? Don't bank on it! In a series on the book of Isaiah at church, I had given my all on chapter 6 – one of the great passages of the Bible. Later that week I saw a piece of paper sticking out of one of the church Bibles in the seats. I pulled it out; it was a Filofax page containing notes that someone had written on my exposition of Isaiah's dramatic call! I have the page in front of me now. There are a few lines of writing, then they tail off into a line sketch of a mouse, a snail and an elephant. Slightly humbling!

Give it some teeth

At some point you have to end. But how? A good rule of thumb is to summarise your main points, then wind up with some words of personal application, challenge or appeal – the talk does need some teeth!

It may, perhaps, be done by alluding to an earlier illustration given; it may be quite helpful to have a kind of sub-theme subtly weaving its way through the talk and popping up at the end. Sometimes a story or word from human experience (including your own) can bring the talk to a sharpened point.

Sometimes the right quotation can do it. I once concluded a radio talk with an illuminating remark from the Gospel singer, George Beverley Shea, given on the occasion of his eightieth birthday. Later that week I heard from a listener who, terrified of what lay in front of him the next day, had happened to switch on his radio just as my talk was finishing. He only got the last sentence! It hit him like a prophecy from heaven as he switched on and heard, *Fear not tomorrow; God is already there*.

That is the point, really. When you have prayed and prepared as best you can, God can take hold of something that was almost incidental to your talk and transform it into a message of divine power for someone in need.

* * * * *

Nothing interprets life like life.

W.E. Sangster.

5

THE ILLUSTRATIONS

In the brightly-lit theatre, the audience has eyes only for the performers on stage. Differently-coloured spotlights cause costumes and dresses to flash and sparkle. As the show comes to a triumphant finish, people cascade out into the night, humming the theme tune. What a drama! What a story!

The story's the thing, of course. The costumes helped, naturally. So did the lighting. But the effects were there, not only for their own sake, but to heighten awareness of the plot. It would be a very poor lighting engineer who caused theatre buffs to exclaim, 'We saw a wonderful show. I forget its name now, but the lighting was magnificent.'

In the exciting challenge of public speaking, the little asides, the newspaper allusions, the illustrations from life, act as shafts of light to heighten and illustrate the mighty central truth – to help it stick in the memory for ever. Illustrations are not there to draw attention to themselves. But when they are used well, they can help our speaking to come alive, to fizz and crackle with interest and imagination.

How to use them

Our supreme model is Christ, the greatest teacher of all. Open up anywhere you like in the Gospel books; his use of metaphor, stories and everyday objects are on every page:

> 'Foxes have holes and birds of the air have nests, but the Son of Man has nowhere to lay his head.'
> 'It is not the healthy who need a doctor, but the sick.'
> 'How can the guests of the bridegroom mourn while he is with them?'
> 'I am sending you out, like sheep among wolves.'
> 'As the weeds are pulled up and burned in the fire, so it will be at the end of the age.'
> 'There was a man who had two sons.'

There is something about a vivid illustration; it earths the truth in something that is familiar to the hearer. It's far more than banging in a joke or story to brighten up the proceedings. It involves your whole approach to language. It requires the ruthless editing out of abstract words like *reciprocal, implemented, options, mortality* and *function*. It is, rather, *getting a feel for speaking in pictures*.

Illustrations give interest to the speaker

You are not just a cardboard cut-out, uttering words; you are a living being who has read, travelled, played sport and known grief. You are part of the same world as your audience. They need to know that.

The Illustrations

Illustrations give clarity to the truth
Take the Resurrection of Jesus Christ. President Richard Nixon's former 'hatchet man' in the White House was Chuck Colson, who, with others, was caught up in the Watergate scandal that took him to prison back in the 1970s. Colson, who became a Christian, then used the lies of Watergate in his defence of the Biblical account of the Resurrection:

> We couldn't hold our stories together for three weeks under that pressure ... I was around the most powerful men in the world, but we couldn't hold the lie. If the Resurrection wasn't true, those disciples could never have held out. No one could do that. Someone would have dug out the tape, or something!
>
> (From *Evangelism Today* magazine).

An apt illustration can highlight something that you are saying and cause the listener to assent inwardly: *Got it.*

Illustrations give edge to the issue
After all, we must be up there at the front as *persuaders*. Speaking once on the theme of Judgment, I illustrated by referring to the cleaning lady who had worked for sixty years at the Kremlin in Moscow – Polina Malinka was her name. She finally broke her silence in December, 1996, and gave to the press her own assessment of the personal habits of her masters, from Stalin to Boris Yeltsin.

It must, I said, have been a little threatening for even the powerful leaders at the Kremlin to have a newspaper publish the revelations of Polina Malinka on their personal habits ... and that's just the *cleaner*! What of Jesus Christ, then, and *his* revelations, which will be shouted from the roof tops on the final day of reckoning?

Sometimes a simple illustration is enough to drive the point home to the conscience and challenge the will.

Illustrations give space to the listeners

Quite often, an illustration comes as a welcome 'breather' in the middle of the talk. I will sometimes use an illustration as a new section of the talk begins. It is there to throw light on what I am about to explain, but it is also there to give a little gesture of relief to any listeners whose concentration has slipped. I am helping them back into the flow once more.

So much for the use of illustrations. But where do they all come from?

How to find them

I think I have good news at this point. Let the illustrations come to you. You do not have to be working overtime on this matter. The illustrations are all around us. Their sources are endless.

There are illustrations from our observation

Shop windows and advertising hoardings make a good start. On coming out from Tom Stoppard's complicated play *Hapgood* one night, I made a note of the newspaper review, blown up on a poster outside, 'You don't have to be an Einstein to understand this play – but it helps.' The plot ... the meaning of life ... the failure of intellect alone to understand God's revelation – it wasn't difficult to make a connection.

The Illustrations

There are illustrations from biography
As I write this chapter, I have just been loaned a biography by a friend. It is David McCullough's best-seller on the former U.S. President Harry Truman. I have only flipped a few pages at random, and found my attention arrested by a photograph of a jubilant Truman, having just won the presidential election, holding up a copy of the *Chicago Tribune*, with its premature headline 'Dewey defeats Truman'. The last laugh ... Victory out of defeat – in a book of over 900 pages. Do you think it will be the only item noted down for future use?

When you read biographies, whether Christian or secular, read them with a pad and ballpoint near at hand.

There are illustrations from life
Sport, family, entertainment, the animal kingdom, politics, human achievement, newspaper clippings – the public speaker has only to develop an eye for the *messages* conveyed by life's happenings, to be assured of a bottomless reservoir of illustrative material.

There are illustrations from history
Don't be content with books of 'gathered' historical allusions and quotations. It is tempting to use them; I have succumbed myself in earlier days. But there is nothing as satisfying, or as authentic, as the historical or literary allusion that you have excavated for yourself from the primary sources. You can then legitimately regard it as 'yours'.

There are illustrations from the Bible itself
There are the prayers of Nehemiah, the frustrations of the Psalmist ('Break their teeth O God'), the courage of

Stephen, the leadership of Deborah, and the exploits of Joshua, Elijah and Esther. The teaching of Jesus himself drew generously on incidents and sayings from the Old Testament, to illustrate a point or to sound an echo in the minds of his listeners. We can do the same.

Let it be emphasised; some speakers give an impression that they are professional 'gatherers' of anecdotes, jokes, stories and quotations. We don't have to do that. Better to be a serious student of the *Bible* – and to let the helpful illustrative matter float in from all sides as we read, eat, walk, socialise and work.

Accepting this, there ought to be ways of catching hold of those illustrations and then saving them for future use.

How to store them

In chapter 3, I highlighted the importance of noting down every illustration as it comes – *and to do it at once*. It is the same with those golden moments of illumination, when we 'see' some aspect of God's truth that until now had always seemed fuzzy and hard to get hold of.

George Frederick Handel is an example in this respect. Who knows what the world would have missed if the great eighteenth century composer had failed to start writing, the moment the idea was born for *The Messiah*? But he obeyed the summons, and the world's most inspiring oratorio was swiftly written down in a breathless twenty-three days.

Moments of overwhelming clarity must be harnessed as they occur. To delay, even by five minutes, may well put the lid on it; half an hour later will find you scratching your head and wondering what it was that had so gripped you.

The Illustrations

Having made a note on a 5 x 3 inches card, I then have to decide how to title the illustration, along the right hand edge, the title thus facing uppermost once the card finds a place in the index system. The guidance is, *Go for the obvious point that the illustration makes.*

Here is an example. Mr. S. L. Potter of La Mesa, California, performed a bungee jump at the age of 100, in October, 1993 – from a 210 foot jump tower, the highest in America. His son, Wally Potter, confessed, 'It almost gave me a heart attack, just watching.' After the jump, Mr. Potter asked for his stick and walked back to his old people's home. The press story was dated October 15th, 1993.

To date, I have not used this little item. Perhaps I never will. But it is there, waiting for me, one of several cards entitled *Old Age*. You will note the anchoring of certain details; name, place, date, the height of the jump. If a card contains a quotation, it is wise to record the source book, publisher and page number. At the very bottom of the item, I will add a single word, *USED*. Under it I will record the place, occasion and date on which I have used the illustration. In this way I can check myself from over-using material before the same people. When I have used an item at our own church, I will even make a record of the actual service I was speaking at.

Speakers will have their tag-words, under which illustrations can be indexed – and cross-indexed as well. Although I will always attempt to give an item its most obvious heading, there may well be secondary topics for which the card will find a use. Let me take as an example, the first of a number of my cards that come under the category of 'The Cross'.

This first card on the Cross, like all my other 'first cards', starts with a clear, blank space simply headed, *See under*. Within this space, over a passage of time, I have tried to include references to cards which *allude* to the Cross, perhaps in some secondary, though relevant way.

Thus, there has been slowly gathered, under the 'See Under' heading, a number of references to other cards. Here are some: *Hope*: (2: Karl Barth quote); *Justice* (1: Timothy Evans); *Evangelism* (8: Festo Kivengere's conversion); *Bible* (21: Pelé's goal), etc. Other more obvious cross-references would include *Love*, *Propitiation*, *Atonement*, *Guilt*, etc.

Laborious? Not really; not if the basic set-up is clear in your mind. The point in all this is that *you will never remember*. If you want to save hours hunting through notebooks, or scanning through biographies, it seems wise, from the very start, to get into the habit of a storage system that can ensure your reading, your observations and experiences are all playing a maximum part in your work as a speaker for the Kingdom of God.

But let us now heed some warnings over the use of illustrations.

How to control them
In the giving of a talk, is there a balance between droning like a lecturer and acting like a clown? I suggest that there is. Beginning with the clowning issue, let's look at the humour.

Let the humour be incidental
The talk that *has* to begin with a joke every time has, in certain circles, very nearly turned into an art-form all of

its own. One can reach the point that the talk has failed if it has not made people laugh. Laughter can indeed create a rapport between speaker and listeners, and can illustrate a point in a very attractive way, but the humour that works best of all is the kind in which it doesn't really *matter* if no one laughs. A point has still been made, albeit in an attractive way. As far as possible let the humorous allusion be original to your own situation and experience. A second rule, then:

Let the illustrations be your own
My advice is not to rely upon jokes out of books, nor to borrow other speakers' stories – they may backfire on you. Books are inevitably read by *others*; Speakers can travel *widely* these days! Never use 'treasures' of collected illustrations. The strong likelihood is that your borrowed item will be familiar to more of your audience than you had anticipated. Stories have the trick of doing the rounds of the social scene and church circuit at alarming speed! I inwardly groan when I hear a speaker starting out on a story the end of which I know all too well. Strive, if you can, to create your own illustrations at first hand. Of course it is always possible, as you read or hear of someone else's experience, that your memory will be triggered about some parallel happening in your own situation. Then some adaptation can be made.

Let all the stories and anecdotes be authenticated
I cannot emphasise this too strongly. It is not to the credit of the fellowship of Christ that a vast 'folklore' of stories is in existence – the origin of which tend to be shrouded in mystery. 'Miracle' stories abound ... but were you there

yourself? Do you know the name of the person who *was* present? Did they tell it to you personally? You saw it in a magazine? Where did the magazine get it from?

There are far too many 'John 3:16' wonder stories on the loose; the soldier on the battlefield, whose Bible stopped the bullet from penetrating his heart, crucially halting at John 3:16 ... but where was it, *Vietman*.... *Flanders*.... In the *Crimea*?! The man in prison who used his gift Bible for paper to roll his cigarettes with; smoking his way through the New Testament until he reached John 3:16 – sometimes he turns up in Cambridge, sometimes in China, Australia, anywhere; he has certainly lasted all of forty years! Let these unauthenticated anecdotes be banned from your talks.

Let personal confidences be kept

A public address is no occasion in which to betray information that was given to you in the course of a private talk – even if you are thousands of miles away from the person in question. An American pastor has written, 'to treat anyone as a theological butterfly, no matter how much care we convey in pinning them to the mounting board and studying marks of identification, is a violation. If we reduce a person to sermon material, we are agents of alienation' (Eugene H. Peterson, *Working the Angles*, Eerdmans).

Apart from anything else, the mere fact of blurting out somebody else's secrets is likely to give rise to the thought among the audience, *If I confide in this speaker, no doubt my own confidences will be cheerfully trotted out in some future meeting*. Naturally the exception to this caution exists in the case of those who have given permission for their intimate story to be told – and it should be stated that this is so. There is also obviously no ban on the telling of someone's story when they themselves have already made it public.

Let the quotations be made from books that we have actually read

Such a habit makes for integrity. I think that we may concede that there can be exceptions to this principle, not least when the original source material is so rare or inaccessible that the speaker has no hope of ever reading the work at first hand. It is possible, however, that friends and supporters may offer to buy you books of 'gathered' quotations; *politely refuse them*. If you should be given such a book, put it high up on the top shelf, and refuse even to be tempted to dip into it for an instant quotation.

Of course we may forgive the novice speaker for grabbing at any and every item, quotation or story in the early days of a speaking career, when the number of books so far read may be very limited. But make the resolve that as you advance, you are going to dig out those helpful quotations for yourself!

In any case, the literary allusion or quotation ought to be *short*. Once it gets beyond thirty words, you will begin to see eyes glaze over. It is the same with poetry; in general poetry should only be used very sparingly; for many listeners it is a real turn-off.

Illustrations ... to a real degree their use is a knack, born out of love of people and a love of life itself. Here is the art of making something out of nothing, of seeing meaning and even divine messages in an object as unassuming as an office cleaner in Moscow.

*****

PART TWO

* * * * *

HOW TO PRESENT

When I went to France I said to Christ: 'I in You and You in me!' and many a time in confronting a laughing, scoffing crowd single-handed, I have said, 'You and I are enough for them. I won't fail You and You won't fail me.'

Kate Booth,
The Maréchale, by James Strahan

Anything worth doing well takes practice. I listen to great pianists, watch the Olympic athletes, hear about surgeons who perform incredible operations. And then I think of the long hours of daily practice over the years that brought them to that place. It is easy to become casual in a land where Christianity is accepted.

Ruth Bell Graham,
Legacy of a Pack Rat, Oliver Nelson.

6

FACING THE AUDIENCE

It was after Christmas, and a note had been pushed under my study door. It was from our next-door neighbour, John Stott. He was due to preach at All Souls in the New Year, from Deuteronomy chapters 1–3. The announced title was *The Key to the Good Life*.

'I would be grateful,' read the note, 'if someone would be kind enough to explain to me what is meant by *The Good Life*, and where in Deuteronomy 1–3, I am expected to find this elusive key.'

Among the church staff we had to smile at this, but the point was made. Even advanced scholars and expositors need a proper briefing and an understanding of expectations before they can stand up with confidence and face an audience. There is nothing like seeing a date and a subject on a programme card – *and your own name against them*!

Of course, it was harder for God's messengers of old:

Then said I, 'Ah, Lord God! behold I cannot speak: for I am a child.' But the Lord said unto me, 'Say not, I am a child: for thou shalt go to all that I shall send thee, and whatsoever I command thee thou shalt speak. Be not afraid of their faces: for I am with thee to deliver thee,' saith the Lord

(Jer. 1:6-8, KJV).

'Their faces' ... that is part of the ordeal. Where are you supposed to *look*? A group of us budding speakers put that question to a renowned exponent many years ago.

'Look at them just below the chin,' he laid down. 'You don't have to be afraid of them. Think of them as sacks of potatoes.'

It might, perhaps, be kindly advice for the first-timer, quivering with fright – but in my heart I disagreed, though I could never have challenged the great man. In all our human communication eye contact is vital; more than that, it's *natural*. Try as I did, I could never force myself to look at people, collar-level.

There are speakers, certainly, who scarcely glance at the audience at all. Their gaze is fixed on a point about five degrees above head level. Result; the oration becomes detached, remote, aloof. The audience might as well not be there at all. There seems to be some *other*, perhaps celestial, audience that the speaker has in view.

But let's go through the requirements of presenting a talk, in greater detail.

The run-up
First, there is the question of your arrival, fully briefed – at the appointed venue and on the right date! Believe me, this can go wrong – at either end of the arrangements. I remember getting out of my car one Sunday afternoon, clutching a large visual-aid that I

had laboriously constructed, ready to sail in for the annual Birthday Meeting of a children's organisation.

Just ahead of me a man emerged from *his* vehicle, struggling with what was obviously an outsize visual-aid. He walked straight up to the building and was admitted.

I looked round cautiously – apparently no one had seen me yet. Rapidly I retraced my steps to the car, bundled in the visual-aid and drove home. Had I got it wrong, or had they? On reflection I think it was a double-booking on *their* part. I never checked back, and they never contacted me. I now had a free talk up my sleeve!

This is part of the run-up. Don't make arrange-ments on the phone; *have some documentation*. The place, the event, the date, time and a phone number for emergencies.

But wise speakers are those who go further and establish the purpose of the talk, the size of the meeting, its age distribution and its very *style*. Is the talk to be given from behind a table, in front of a table, from a lectern? All these factors will have a direct bearing upon the content and approach of your address, its emphasis and its length – and even the clothes that you should be wearing. I wouldn't like to turn up in a suit and tie, and find myself in the middle of a barbecue.

Talking of ties, if the occasion requires one, I will wear a tie that doesn't attract attention. It's part of the spir-itual preparation. It's the *message* and its divine author that should be the magnet, not the messenger! For the same reason, when it comes to Sunday ministry at our church I will nearly always wear the *same tie* week after week. The dress of the messenger, while in keeping with the surroundings, ought not to be of the kind that ex-cites comment!

Further, just as the dress should be tailored to the occasion, so should the speaker's *notes*. To be sure, I have my basic format for regular speaking, but there are occasions when a small jotter pad would be more suitable for a particular occasion.

In one instance, when I was an after-dinner speaker, I could not quite risk having *no* notes (as I would have preferred). Instead I wrote some notes on the back of the invitation card. It seemed a reasonably natural gesture to pull the card out of my pocket at the start, remind the company of the advertised topic of my address, and then simply to keep the card in my hand for the rest of the talk as an *aide-memoir*.

Here you are now in the room. You have met the organisers; you have made friends with the caretaker and – if you are wise – you will, if time permits, make yourself known to one and another of the audience. This last adds a real added-value dimension to the occasion. It establishes that you are not just a platform performer, but that you genuinely like people. It also helps you with the pre-talk nerves – *why, these are just ordinary people*.

Meeting your listeners in person may, indeed, change some aspect or other of your talk. For my mother it once changed her *entire* talk, as a member of the group confided to her, 'I'll never forget your wonderful talk to us *last* year – you spoke on The Woman at the Well!' Somewhere my mama had slipped up and had prepared the same subject again!

But now it's time. You are as physically, mentally and spiritually ready as you are ever going to be for this one. The meeting so far may have seemed like an eternity to you, but the run-up is over, and your turn has come. You pray quietly and you get up! The ambassador of the Kingdom doesn't slouch. God's messenger *stands*.

On your feet

Just *before* you get up, you check the time on your watch. I usually make a mental note; by the time the big hand on my watch is pointing to a certain figure, I ought to be winding up the talk. I will, during the course of the talk, give myself further time-checks. There is no need to be ostentatious about this. If the audience can *see* the speaker checking the time, you can be sure that a good half of them will follow suit! No point in distracting attention; twist your watch round so that its face is on the *inside* of your wrist. That way you won't have to make any telltale movement.

What happens first? Much depends on the nature of the gathering. An opening prayer (or does the prayer come later)? Words of appreciation for being invited to speak? Or straight in? The inexperienced speaker, in particular, needs to get this worked out in anticipation of the occasion. *Write it out if necessary.*

The fact is that a great opportunity is presented to you in those first twenty seconds on your feet. So take your time over it. Too many speakers (far too many speakers) start gabbling while the audience (or congregation) is still adjusting position. *Wait*, till the rustling and fidgeting have abated and all eyes are turned on you. Then is the chance to see if, by the grace of God, you can grab the attention for him and his Word.

There are only two notable exceptions that I can think of, with regard to waiting for attention. The first is in the case of a meeting where the place has gone mad and is about to teeter out of control. This can happen in certain children's events, or young people's happenings, or on occasions in prisons. In such instances it may be wiser to charge straight in.

The second exception is in the case of a meeting that has gone to sleep! Everything is soporific, boring and flat. A new dynamic is needed, and you are the one to provide it. *Begin at once*, cheerfully, buoyantly and with gusto. On occasions I have started talking even before I had reached the speaker's place, so concerned was I to wake the room up!

Imagine that the room *is* awake and with you. You've got started. How is the talk going?

In mid-flight

There comes a point in a talk that is going well, where you are no longer listening to your own voice. You have got into your stride and are now 'focused' on your listeners, their needs, and what GOD may be saying to them. You see that guy near the door, the one with the green sweater? You've never met him, but, who knows, perhaps he is in a quandary of which you know nothing.

Believe that God is using you. You see that woman in the far, far corner? The one with the specs and the beads? Are you sure that your voice is carrying to her over there? Just increase the decibels a little ... in case. *Help me, Lord. May your Spirit take these words and –*

Crash! A window bangs open suddenly. Thirty-five heads turn round simultaneously. Pity – it's the *exact* moment when I was about to give that marvellous illustration that makes the whole thing clear. O well, just plough on with it regardlessly. *No*. Delaying tactics are called for! Normally you should *never* pad, but at this moment, PAD! *Keep* padding; that's better, the heads are turning back to me again. Are they back on track? *Now* let go with the illustration!

Time check. Wow, the minutes are flying by. I'll skip story No. 1 and opt for story No. 2, with its lead in to my application and the quotation that I've been saving to the end. And a prayer ... and ... and ... *sit down*. O Lord, thank you, thank you.

Aftermath

Quite often the real work of the talk begins when it is over. Stick around! Stick around at the *front*, where people can still see you. If you had been on a platform, however, get *off* the platform, and onto a level with everybody else. The only speakers who genuinely must be whisked away from the building are those few men and women whose international ministry has brought them into touch with so many people that they need a measure of protection if they are not to collapse from exhaustion.

But you and I are not of that breed. Woe betide the speakers with an inflated view of their influence, thinking of themselves as mega-performers and their fellow-Christians as simply 'the punters' at the event in which they are starring. Nor can any true Christian leader afford to fall victim to the *we/them* syndrome, viz:

> If *we* do this at that certain point in the meeting ... if *we* put on that special piece of music ... if *we* use *this* technique, it will make *them* react in *that* desirable way.

Is that the way of the servant of Christ, the Servant of all? No, it is the way of the cynical manipulator; of the sectarian on an egotistical balloon-ride in which precious people are viewed only as 'punters', as gate-fodder to swell the coffers and inflate the image.

You are one of them, so ... stick around! There may be someone who will want to speak with you, confide in you, or to have you pray for them. In secret prayer, ask Christ at the end of the talk whether there is anything *else* he would have you do for him?

And then ... what about praise? The plaudits that may come your way? At times they will come. There are three things we can do with them. First, *accept them* with grace. People mean to encourage us, and we can receive those words at their face value. But secondly we can *divert them* to their rightful destination. Corrie Ten Boom, who became world-famous after triumphantly surviving terrible ordeals in World War II, was able to deal with the congratulations that poured upon her, by treating each one as she would the gift of a flower. Then at the end of the day she would 'hand' what had become by now a bouquet of tributes to Jesus Christ. 'Lord, these are for you!' she would pray.

A third thing we may do with kind tributes is to *temper them* with constructive criticisms from friends whom we can trust to tell us of ways of improving our speaking.

We ought to take the chance of hearing our talks on cassette, or seeing them on video. Pop singers do it, because they know that they must keep raising their standards. Should we be content with less?

... So you're on your way back? I would hazard that you feel *better*, more fulfilled than you did on coming out today? We can relate that to the filling of the Holy Spirit. As we obey the Lord in service, so he fills. The way to be filled is to be emptied!

And the things that might have been done better? There's always a next time!

*****

Curate: 'Are you suggesting, Vicar, that I put more fire into my sermons?'

Vicar: 'No, I'm really trying to suggest that you put more of your sermons into the fire.'

7

SPEAKING THAT GLOWS

'Is *normal* good enough?'

The speaker was John Chapman of Sydney, Australia. He was leading a seminar for church leaders, and I was among them. I doubt if there was a delegate in the room who would have conceded that 'normal' could ever be good enough, where speaking for God was concerned.

It's teasing and tantalising at the same time.

'Every occasion's got to be like an ace down the centre line!' I urge upon my speaking colleagues and myself. It is a hard thing to pull off, in our media-driven society where the television sound-bite supposedly marks the limit of a listener's attention-span.

And yet! The contention of this book is that when the Christian fellowship at large recovers its confidence in the age-old teaching of the Scriptures, appetites will grow, heads will pop up and people will *listen*.

And lives will be changed.

It was as if a light suddenly turned on and everything became clear. I was, quite frankly, speechless when I came up to speak afterwards.

Speaking in Public - Effectively

I stumbled into church quite spontaneously one Sunday evening in January, to find John Chapman speaking - I certainly wasn't prepared to be so violently challenged! It is the best thing that has happened to me.

As a lieutenant in the U.S. Marine Corps, having survived leading my unit in battle, I listened one Sunday morning to words that captured me, from Philippians 3. I left in stunned silence, and later, flat on my back in bed, I said to God, 'I'm yours'.

As an Indian Brahmin, I felt as though great weights were being lifted off me.

Perhaps rather late (I am 63), I have become a Christian. I do not believe words could convey the inspiration and effect the message had upon me - it has happened like a thunderclap!

It seems like the most natural thing in the world, as if you were coming home.

Statements like these can be duplicated all over the world. What lies behind them is a principle that is as simple as it is profound. Let me set it out boldly:

SPEAKING GLOWS WITH LIFE-TRANSFORMING ENERGY WHEN BOTH SPEAKER AND LISTENERS ARE AWARE THAT ANOTHER VOICE HAS TAKEN OVER.

Speaking that Glows

The moment we recognise this truth, it is obvious that such a phenomenon cannot be contrived. No speaker can *make* it happen. It remains a remarkable fact, however, that it can happen for inexperienced public speakers whose training and education may be minimal; whereas plenty of learned discourses have been delivered which, as John Wesley observed after a visit to Glasgow, *contained much truth, but were no more likely to awaken one soul than an Italian opera* (*Wesley's Journals*, May 15th, 1774).

Many years ago there was a remarkable missionary and evangelist by the name of Kate Booth, the daughter of the celebrated founder of the Salvation Army. Fragile and young, she and her band of sister Salvationists were given great success as they sang and witnessed in the taverns and brothels of Paris. There Kate became dubbed *La Maréchale*.

Years later, an English bishop, John Taylor Smith, asked an attender at one of her meetings, 'Why do you all flood to hear the Maréchale?'

The answer was enlightening.

'We have never heard anyone who made Jesus so real before. She brought Him right to us. He was there. He was speaking to you. You were touching Him, and His love was enveloping you. His purity and His power seemed to burn through you. It was preaching such as we had never heard in our lives before'

(*The Heavenly Witch*, Carolyn Scott, Hamish Hamilton).

He was speaking to you. That is the phenomenon exactly. They knew all about this in the New Testament. The apostle Paul puts it vividly when he tells his readers (none of whom had ever seen or heard Christ):

But ye have not so learned Christ; if so be *that ye have heard him*, and have been taught by him....

(Eph. 4:20f., KJV).

It is a pity that modern versions have mistranslated the Greek to read 'Surely you heard *about* him', but the King James version has it right. The people of Ephesus had only heard *preachers*, but the apostle says that the person they heard was Jesus!

Whenever and wherever it happens, the result is that there is a *refreshment* in the speaking – and the listeners will want to come *back*. They haven't had to be coerced or worked upon by the speaker; no special antics were necessary. There was an immediacy and a compulsion about the message.

George Whitefield's speaking in the eighteenth century compelled attention, in contrast to the arid essays delivered by many of his contemporaries. A landowner, famous for his forestry projects, was sternly taken to task by an eminent cleric for going to listen to the 'Enthusiast' Whitefield. The forester protested, 'When I hear *you*, I am planting trees all the time! But during the whole of Mr. Whitefield's sermon, I had no time for planting even *one*!'

In an article on 'the dying art of rhetoric', David McKie made the observation that today's decline in political oratory 'may have something to do with the decline of organised religion':

The parallels are many and inescapable. The huge crowds to whom Gladstone preached, and his tireless journeys to reach them, recall the great non-conformist preachers,

Wesley and Whitefield.... The language of nineteenth century politicians, too, is full of allusions to religion. Often, in its cadences and love of repetition, it has a specifically biblical ring.

(*Observer Review*, March 23rd, 1997)

McKie had a point. When a biblical world-view ceases to exert an effective hold on the public, the result across society will be a *narrowing* of the boundaries of life and politics; a *reduction* of civilisation's burning issues to the limited 'general interest' level of housing, pensions, tax relief and petrol prices. With such restricted horizons, is it surprising if political rhetoric is in decline?

This affects the church too. It is only as the giant themes of *Creation*, *the Fall*, *Redemption* and the *End Times* become once again a mighty scaffolding around the thinking of Christians, that their speakers can dare to hope for a new relevance and glow in all their utterances. Jesus made the point that it is the pagan world that makes food and welfare the focal point of life; that this is an empty and futile quest. Seek first the Kingdom of God, he emphasised, 'and all these things (housing, hospitals etc.) will be given to you as well' (Matt. 6:31-33). Such things are only a valuable by-product of higher priorities; life does not begin and end with *them*.

There will be a glow and a captivation about our messages when the speaker and the audience can share together in their awareness that they are caught up in something that is infinitely bigger than themselves. On the purely secular front we have an example of this principle in Shakespeare's *Henry V*. On the eve of the battle of Agincourt, the King rallies his troops and treats them as brother colleagues, as part of a momentous epic:

We few, we happy few, we band of brothers;
For he today that sheds his blood with me
Shall be my brother; be he ne'er so vile,
This day shall gentle his condition:
And gentlemen in England now a-bed
Shall think themselves accurst they were not here;
And hold their manhoods cheap whiles any speaks
That fought with us upon St. Crispin's day.

But the eternal Kingdom of God is bigger than any of this. It is going to outlast every institution going. Let this thought be part of your preparation as you get ready to face your audience! All over the world this Kingdom is growing, in the lives of millions of Christ's followers.

'I felt it was just for me.'
     'You'll never know how much your talk helped me.'
     'All right, your talk has convinced me! How do I now get started?'

These and other sentences are going to be said to you many times in your speaking career. Each testimony you will treasure; you will never get used to it. Indeed you will gasp with wonderment that your speaking could ever make a dent in anything or anybody. It is the glory of the Gospel that God has chosen to work in this way:

Speaking that Glows

For God, who said, 'Let light shine out of darkness,' made his light shine in our hearts to give us the light of the knowledge of the glory of God in the face of Christ.

But we have this treasure in jars of clay to show that this all-surpassing power is from God and not from us
(2 Cor. 4:6-7).

The point must be repeated; there is no way in which the touch of God upon our speaking can be manufactured or simulated. This entire mystery is under the domain of the Spirit of God. He is Lord. He comes in power upon the service of Christ's representatives as and when he will.

Some have referred to this work as the Anointing of the Spirit upon the minister of Christ. They will urge that we seek such an anointing before we speak for the Lord. It is certainly right that every time I speak for God I should be spiritually prepared, my sins forgiven, my message ready and my heart claiming the filling of God's Holy Spirit for the task ahead.

In point of fact, however, as a Christian, I have already *been* 'anointed' for Christ's service, the day I became his follower. Once we are past Pentecost, all the verbs concerning our *initiation* into the life of the Spirit are in the past tense. Evidently, as a Christian, I have been anointed for God's service (2 Cor. 1:21)

It is true that for the *development* of life in the Spirit, there is plenty that we must attend to; we should not *grieve* the Spirit, we are to *walk* in him, and we should be *filled* with the Spirit every day. But I do not see that there is some indispensable and separate 'anointing' that is to be sought, on top of that which was already given. Thus having done the preparation, both of our message and ourselves, we are to go ahead and speak in the authority and Name of Christ ... *and leave it to the sovereign Spirit to touch and speak to whom he will.* It is finally up to him.

But that established, there is no call for a speaker to be careless or lazy about this reliance on the Spirit to move in power. We are to see to it that our own hard work and personal preparation provide the Spirit of God with a mouthpiece that is pleasing to him.

As I understand it, speaking that is irradiated with the presence of God has, as its background, prayer, meditation, love, grace and suffering. Again it must be emphasised that no amount of natural ability can cover for their absence. You cannot simply pull the notes of an old talk out of a file, walk to the platform *and act the professional*, with any assurance that the inspiration of heaven will be in your words – no matter how impressive your show of sanctity and spiritual readiness.

Eugene Peterson, writing from a Presbyterian ministry in Bel Air, Maryland, declares, 'I don't know of any other profession in which it is quite as easy to fake it, as in ours' (*Working the Angles*, Eerdmans).

The other side of this should encourage the easily depressed among us. Many will be the occasions when, like the English missionary of old, Henry Martyn, you look at the notes of your talk and echo with him, '*I was chilled and frozen by the stupidity of it.*' But then comes the surprise:

'I can't thank you enough for speaking to my situation.'
'I found your words so encouraging.'

Speaking that Glows

'How can I get a copy of your talk? I so want to go over it again.'

Can this happen, even through my speaking? That is the experience that has astonished a long succession of speakers ahead of you. Yes, it can happen. You cannot *make* it happen. Nevertheless there will be moments during the course of a day, or perhaps in the night, when your own thinking on some point becomes lit up with an overwhelming clarity. *Don't let that moment go*. Don't wait for even ten seconds. The Kikuyu of East Africa call such thoughts *Meciria*; they use the word to describe deep, imaginative penetrating thoughts. Such 'thoughts' must be dwelt upon, harnessed – and written down as fast as they come. A five-minute delay may be fatal. Where did they come from, unbidden, into your consciousness? Out of something that you heard or saw? Out of a group Bible study? In the middle of your prayer time?

Naturally, these *meciria* must be checked against the yardstick of Scripture. But again and again we shall find to our joy that the Holy Spirit will be pleased to use God-given flashes of insight and imagination to highlight the meaning of a great Bible truth to the lasting benefit of our hearers.

Don't be content with 'normal'. The world could do with a new generation of *speakers*, whom God can use to lift the veil from the minds of undiscerning people – to reveal a world and a universe glowing with meaning.

*****

Some are for ever playing tenor, lifting up their hands with exultation, jingling their shrill bells. Others play nothing but bass, always grumbling and growling. Don't you hear that Eolian harp, my brother, its strings swept by the breeze, its melody gentle yet strong, varied yet harmonious? That is what the Christian Ministry ought to be – the genuine impartial Scripture played upon and applied under a divine influence – under the breath of heaven.

Charles Simeon, by H.C.G. Moule, Christian Focus.

8

YOUR UNIQUE TRADEMARK -
THE VOICE

'Right, Mr. Bewes. Would you kindly take this Prayer Book and read the opening exhortation for *Morning Prayer* – as though you were leading the service.'

I was in Cambridge, studying for the ordained ministry at Ridley Hall college. Mr. Duxbury, the elocutionist was with us for his annual visit, putting each of us through our paces. He was rather deaf. Gingerly I took the prayer book and started off as impressively as I could:

Dearly beloved brethren, the Scripture moveth us in sundry places to acknowledge and confess our manifold sins and wickedness; and that we should not dissemble nor cloak them before the face of Almighty God our heavenly Father; but confess them with an –

'*Stop!*' commanded my guru.
I looked up anxiously.
'What's the matter with you?' enquired Mr. Duxbury. 'What's troubling you?'

'Oh ... no, nothing. Was I doing it wrong?'

'I was only wondering! Why that funny voice? It sounded so unnatural, so *forced*. It occurred to me that you'd suddenly had a personality change!'

'Oh, well no. I was trying to read it with meaning.'

'Meaning, eh? What's the meaning of the word *dissemble*, then?'

'Er, well, it means to dispute something, to disagree.'

'It does not. It means to deceive by not saying enough. You'll need to know the meaning of what you're saying, to start with, if you're to have a hope of getting across to a congregation.'

I remained silent. What was coming next?

'Now, Mr. Bewes. You're the executive of a company, giving his report to the Annual Meeting. You are about to address the shareholders. Your obvious opening sentence will begin with the words *Mr. Chairman, ladies and gentlemen*. Think yourself into that meeting. Now how are you going to say it?'

I took a breath.

'Mr. Chairman, ladies and gentlemen!'

'Right!' said Mr. Duxbury. '*Quite right*. Now take up that prayer book again. There are people, real people in front of you there. In their own way *they* are shareholders. They have a stake in the church. Start again with that opening exhortation to worship.'

I held the book steady.

'Dearly beloved brethren! the Scripture mov....'

BANG! Mr. Duxbury had hit the table. I jumped.

'*Good*, Mr. Bewes. Very good. If you can keep that *natural* approach in your leading and speaking, you'll be a credit to me! Don't want any parsonic voices in the church, do we? Now kindly read aloud for me the greatest story ever told. Here it is, Luke 15. It's a *story*, remember. Off you go....'

Ridley Hall did many good things for me, but my lesson with Mr. Duxbury was the best-spent forty minutes of my two years in that college. I only wish I could have learnt better from him. I feel deeply indebted to him for saving me from at least some of the pitfalls of public speaking.

What areas should concern us when it comes to the voice?

Voice care

Your voice, like your fingerprint, is unique. It's your trademark. You can be speaking, out of sight, and people will know you by your voice. 'It's only me,' you say, as your acquaintance at the other end picks up the telephone receiver. 'Hullo, Ken!' comes the reply. 'Hullo, Jane!' Once heard, never forgotten!

You will have the same voice all your life. It may perhaps deepen a little over the years, but it need not necessarily become cracked. Many people sound pretty much the same at fifty as they did at twenty-five. Some hold the youthful quality of their voice right into their seventies. Especially if they don't smoke.

Speakers, like singers, need to keep the voice *exercised*. If you speak regularly, you will notice the difference if you have a holiday, and fulfil no speaking engagements for three or four weeks; there will be a loss of power when you get up to speak again. Singers know this. When they are going through their scales, they are doing no more nor less with the voice than the athlete is with bodily exercises. We speakers must take account of this, if our voices are to gain in penetration and flexibility.

'Yes, yes, yes, YES!' boomed Billy Graham's voice in the back of the car as it headed towards the stadium.

'No, no, no, No!' teased Ruth, sitting beside him.

'Yes, *yes*, *YES*, YES!' came the rejoinder.

It was all part of the preparation of body, spirit *and voice* for the service of God.

'Your voice is like a muscle and it needs exercise,' said Mr. Graham during a question and answer session in Amsterdam. Three thousand evangelists had sent in their questions, and he was patiently responding. 'Treat your voice with respect,' he continued. 'I never drink cold water before speaking. It seems to freeze up my vocal chords. If I drink anything it might be a little warm tea.'

Me, I don't drink water, and I only drink tea if it is available in a pre-meeting buffet. But for big occasions, when I want to make sure that the little voice will carry, I will take a couple of pinches of salt about ten minutes before speaking. It seems to get me lubricated. It irons out any kinks that can cause the voice to 'catch' or seize up. Gargling with warm salt water is similarly recommended by some. The great thing to avoid before speaking is *nuts*. They can cause great trouble. Also to be avoided are chocolate, coffee and milky products that can take the edge off the vocal chords. And not a drop of alcohol.

I have one cure, and one cure only for hiccups! I am hardly ever afflicted, but if I were to begin a hiccup attack while waiting to speak, I have found that a teaspoonful of granulated white sugar cures me in five seconds flat. Because I undertake a fair amount of speaking I do, as a matter of fact, keep a small sachet of sugar always with me, in my wallet. I can only remember needing it once, shortly before speaking - but I was glad it was there!

But let's move on to the *power* of the voice.

Voice projection

Whether the voice you were born with is big or little, there is a great deal than can be done to increase its power. It is not that the speaker must ever shout; even the best open-air exponents don't shout. But we need to *project,* and as vibrantly as possible. Three questions!

How are you breathing?

Many speakers breathe far too shallowly, and not into the 'bottom' of their lungs. You should be able to sense that your breathing is being done by what feels like the 'tummy'. How can you encourage yourself to breathe in this way? Peter Westland suggests this exercise:

Get down on your hands and knees and pant like a dog. I know it sounds rather rude, but that is the best way to describe the exercise. Pant quickly but evenly. You will notice it is difficult, while on your hands and knees, to breathe into your chest; the exercise more or less forces you to breathe abdominally.

Teach Yourself Public Speaking,
English Universities Press, Ltd., London.

Having established how to breathe in this way, learn to do it while you are standing, and indeed at all times.

You may need to repeat Peter Westland's exercise until you find yourself beginning to breathe naturally in the normal course.

The reason why your speaking will benefit from correct breathing is this: speaking is the result of a flow of exhaled air passing across the vocal chords. The greater the *power* of the exhalation, the greater the depth, control and steadiness of the voice; the greater also its stamina.

The inclination of the spiritually-minded may be to push all this aside, in their passionate desire for the top priority – to interpret God's message with utter purity. That indeed *is* the top priority. It is, however, worth remembering that the apostle Peter was evidently heard by at least three thousand people on the day of Pentecost; life on the stormy Sea of Galilee must have taught him how to breathe naturally and to speak up! Here is the second question:

What is your mouth doing?
It is fascinating how often we read of the apostles in the book of Acts, that they *opened their mouth and spoke*. Why does Luke need to tell us that they opened their mouths? Surely it is because they were quite obviously in proclamation mode. You cannot proclaim *anything* if your mouth is nearly closed. Try saying 'Coca-Cola' in a way that *projects* – with your teeth nearly together. Then try it with your mouth wide open. The difference in volume and sheer voice quality is staggering. Shouldn't 'open-mouth speech' be something of a way of life, then, for the public speaker? The Africans will find this easier to put into practice than many of the rest of us; they seem to be naturals at it. The Americans are not bad. We British have some way to go! Now, thirdly:

Are you standing properly?

Standing, I must emphasise, not sitting. To stand indicates something of purposefulness, of respect to the audience – and authority. You have been charged with a message, and you are standing up to deliver it. But the breathing, too, will be deeper if you stand.

The speaker needs to be standing in a way that does not prevent the voice from reaching out to all parts of the auditorium. If your hands, for example, are resting on a table in front of you, your body is likely to be leaning forward and down; as a result your breathing will be that much constricted. Similarly, if your head is bending low over scarcely readable notes, the voice is unlikely to be at its most communicative.

My own rule is, keep the feet a little apart (that discourages me from standing on one leg), head up, and – when I remember – shoulders down, and head free to range around the audience. But on, now, to the matter of your voice's range and control.

Voice modulation

Part of me simply advises, *work it out for yourself*. My reason is that a speaker's delivery should never be forced into an unnatural mode. I know a fine young speaker whose voice is naturally phlegmatic in tone; the pitch is unvarying and even. Some might go further and say that it was a little 'flat'. But the ring of sincerity and Christ's love carries this speaker through with great commendation to the hearers. No elocutionist would want to tamper with such an effective instrument.

Besides, we might argue, isn't there a danger that our speaking could degenerate into the putting on of a performance, into mere *acting*? The artificial feeling after that 'elusive' word, when you are already perfectly aware of what you are intending to say, has something of the cringe factor about it.

Yet there is a world of difference between gauche oratorical tricks and *good timing*, between a studied performance and *excellent projection*. Knowing the difference is a key factor in our ensuring that the enduring Word of God is effectively communicated to the greatest number of people possible.

Modulation, the pitch, variation in pace – these can all afford to be worked on – including by the phlegmatics among us. What is your voice doing to the listeners? Is it grabbing their attention, lulling them to sleep, beating them into dullness, or driving them to distraction?

Charles Simeon, whose fifty years of preaching left its mark on Cambridge and on the whole of England, never hesitated to mimic his preaching colleagues, in order to bring about their cure.

'How did I speak this evening?' asked a clerical friend shortly after leaving Simeon's pulpit.

'Why, my dear brother,' came the reply, 'I am sure you will pardon me – you know it is all love, my brother – but indeed it was as if you were knocking on a warming-pan – tin, tin, tin, tin, without any intermission!' (*Charles Simeon*, H. C. G. Moule, Christian Focus).

Perhaps we may follow Simeon's lead and engage in a little gentle mimicry ourselves – always, as he insisted, in love! Can you recognise yourself in any of these cameos?

The Whine

Nothing is ever right with the world, with the church, with the audience! Look at the terrible state of the country. And oh, the standards! And the *bishops*! Of *course* no one is going to church any more; can we *wonder*? Indeed why are *you* in church, with your low prayer life, your feeble giving, your non-existent witness? Unless we wake up to evangelism there won't *be* any church in twenty years time! Moan, moan, moan.

'So *challenging*,' the members say to one another loyally, as they leave the ministrations of the whiner. Have some tea. And a biscuit. We need to recover from this drizzle of depression.

The Drone

It's all on one note, unvarying. The stuff is excellent, but I came in tired; this is sending me into another world. What was that? God's blessings of the New Covenant? I agree. I don't believe I've ever noticed that little laurel wreath on the ceiling before. What made the architect put it into his design, I wonder? There's another one. And another. Well, well, we live and we learn. What's that? The high priest could only go into the Holy of Holies once a year. But then with the tearing of the curtain in Matthew 27.... Oh, my poor back.

The Bark

It's good, of course. But nearly every sentence ends on an upward note that makes me feel vaguely as if I'm in the dock, a bit of a dimwit, and a fool. Why so patronising? There it is again, a rising, accusing pitch that puts me down:

'What God wants is not your possessions, but *yourselves*!

Yeah, yeah, okay, I heard you. There it goes again:

'It's not much good, is it, for Christians to be divided against each other, grouped into rival camps, when there's a dead Society all *around* them!

And yet again:

'So it isn't simply a Gospel with Jewish overtones that Paul describes here; It's no Gospel *at all*! Don't you see that the free grace of God has been put into *reverse*! And it wasn't that Paul had received his message from anybody *else*; it was a revelation from Jesus Christ *himself*!'

Well, he's pretty good, I suppose. But somehow his tone indicates that he *knows* he's good.

The Moo
Not much incisiveness here; it's rather like having a warm bath – or am I by a rippling stream, with the cows lowing in the meadow nearby? It's soothing on the whole, teetering on the antiquarian and senti-mental, and presented with a *rounded* voice with about as much edge imparted to it as a poached egg. It is given with godly sincerity, but I'm falling asle-e-ep....

So. Can you take in this glorious and sublime truth? It's become impressed upon my soul during these days, these precious days of the Mission. It's the *grace*, the rich and *overflowing* grace; the grace that moved the cobbler Bunyan, the grace that awoke the seafaring John Newton, the grace that impelled the reforming Earl of Shaftesbury. It was grace, such grace. O-o-h, the gra-a-ace ....

The cadences rise and fall in a sleep-inducing rhythm that really belongs to an earlier age. But should it even have belonged there?

And what about the soft 'rounded' voice? Believe that God will use it. He will! We need such voices. At the same time, *work on it* a little, as did Demosthenes of old; training yourself to increase your volume above that expected in someone's living room. Do those breathing exercises, and see if you can't get to the point where you can speak with a degree of penetration into a crowded room without amplification.

The Gallop

Ideas, words and thoughts jostle for inclusion in this helter-skelter of a talk. Some of the things said are magnificent, but they are given no space in which to stand out amid the non-stop torrent of gobbled, half-finished words. The mind of the speaker races ahead of the sentence – which is barely finished before the next thought rushes in like an express train. As John Chapman once put it in a preachers' seminar: 'Some talks call to mind the ballad about old MacDonald's Farm. Only in this case it's *Here a thought, there a thought, everywhere a thought, thought*!'

In such an address, the main thread is lost in a tangle of undisciplined verbiage that is very tiring to listen to:

Justification is like saying Just-as-if-I'd never sinned or Just-as-if-I'd died, it changed Martin Luther's whole life, there was that time when it seemed that all Luther's sins were being written down on a great list by the Devil who was accusing ... that's what he's called in the book of Revelation, he's the Accuser of the brethren, so that we're under pressure aren't we all over the world, but it's the truth of Justification about us being accepted and without blame as far as God is concerned, I wish every one of us could grasp....

When a speaker is under a time constraint, the tendency to gabble is accentuated – and I recognise myself as a naturally fast speaker. The cure lies perhaps in two directions; first to shorten the amount of material being crammed into the talk – by as much as a third – and secondly to write out in a full script everything that you are going to say, *every word*, stories, asides and all! Leave ample space on the notes between the beginning and end of each sentence, and underline the words that ought to be accentuated in your delivery. That discipline alone will help to correct the faults and will eventually free you up.

It is possible to think of other cameos, but we must close this chapter with some final observations:

Voice amplification

Some of the old-style preachers used to complain that the arrival of the microphone and amplifier had ruined good speaking. I disagree. It has changed nothing. If you have a voice that naturally projects well into a room, my advice is that you should continue to speak at normal pitch – *as though the microphone wasn't there*.

The microphone and amplifier are only there in order to give some 'lift' to a voice that might not otherwise be easily heard by every part of the audience. These facilities are not provided in order to do the job for you! Many speakers are under the quite erroneous impression that once they are provided with a microphone, all that is required of them is that they should 'chat' as though speaking to someone a yard away, and all will be well.

Keep that little voice 'up'! Mentally we should be addressing our words as though addressing the very back row of listeners. If we are breathing properly, it will be possible to project well and still sound natural.

While, then, we should not be microphone-conscious, there is, however, another part of the public speaker's mindset that should be *aware* of the microphone. It is a matter of consistency of the sound that is coming through to the audience. The talk will suffer if there is a sudden drop in volume, as you turn your head momentarily to the side of the room, or as you step back for a second during your delivery.

I do not mean for a moment that the speaker should *not* have eye contact with people at the side of the room. I only urge that when we do look to the side, there should be developed within us an instinct that takes account of the microphone's existence. Learn to develop the little knack of so adjusting your bodily position when you do turn to the side that automatically you will be speaking *across* the microphone, and not away from it. It has become such an instinctive habit with me that I no longer think about it.

Some speakers enthusiastically advocate the use of the lapel microphone or alternatively the halter microphone that is placed around the neck, so setting them free to turn their heads or even wander around the platform. They are certainly very useful. But if I am given the choice, I will usually opt for the fixed stand microphone; there is less chance of my hand or tie accidentally brushing it. And if I want to cough, it is possible to step back from the fixed microphone. Somehow the lapel or halter microphone imprisons you just a little.

If I am given the choice I will never use a radio microphone. The technology is improving all the time, but there is a great difference in the quality of these microphones. Many of them crackle and pop; they can run out of battery – I have seen too many disasters take place! I got the point when I was asked by the sound and vision technicians in a superb American auditorium, whether I preferred to use the fixed mike or the radio facility.

'O, the fixed mike!' I replied immediately. They beamed their approval. I keep waiting for the day when radio microphones show a marked and uniform improvement all round, but on an outside trip only in September 2001 in front of 400 people I found myself (yet again) let down by a radio mike that I had been assured was of 'terrific quality!'

Meanwhile you have your own, personal, built-in and God-given amplification system. Many speakers never work on their voice at all. We should work on it, and treat it with respect. I used to sing a little chorus when I was a child:

Your Unique Trademark - The Voice

Mine are the hands to do the work,
My feet shall run for Thee;
My lips shall sound the glorious news,
Lord here am I, send me!

God has no voice but ours. In some small way we can trust that the way in which we speak will be worthy of the magnificence of the message that is ours to transmit.

*****

Remember that men and women are not converted, finally, by your sagacity, oratory, theological brilliance or homiletical skill. God in his mercy may use all these and many more gifts. But only God is able to bring people to himself. That is ample incentive to prayer.

D.A. Carson, *The Gagging of God*, Apollos, IVP.

9

SPEAKING FOR A VERDICT

I was playing the guitar ... in the blazing sunshine of Africa. Word had somehow got out, on my speaking trip, that I could play!

'Play the guitar?' I had argued. 'Well, I can just about do the three-chord trick, I suppose. I can also whistle through my teeth if that's any good to you!'

Presently a microphone had been rigged up, and I was doing my turn under a thorn tree by the side of a dusty road that led into the city.

On which are you resting, the rock or the sand?
You'd better make up your mind!
With Christ as foundation your building will stand,
But have you made up your mind?

I felt a little ridiculous out there, interspersing my music with some wayside Gospel chat – but I had an audience! At one point a large bus swung round the corner, crammed with passengers. There was a squeal of brakes as the driver pulled to a standstill. Heads popped out.

'Keep going,' murmured my sponsors encouragingly. I went on obediently:

It's not an easy road; we are travelling to heaven; F o r many are the thorns on the way ....

This is Africa, I reflected. However would this have been received in, say, *Birmingham*? I risked a peep out of the corner of my eye. The bus driver showed not the slightest inclination to move on. Heads were still craning in our direction. Meanwhile my companions were at the side of the bus, busily distributing Christian literature and speaking with the passengers. Every pamphlet was accepted. A full fifteen minutes later the bus rumbled leisurely on its way again. It would have stayed longer if my little stock of songs hadn't been exhausted!

Later I remembered the words of D.L. Moody of Chicago: 'Music and the Bible are the two most important agencies with which to reach the world.'

Certainly this has proved true on numerous occasions. Any of us who speak should not fail to harness what we say to the efforts of our musical colleagues, whether in the context of concerts, celebrations or simply the familiarity of church on Sunday.

Work hard on the music. It's an emotive field, because we are all subject to our own tastes. But try and look at it from others' point of view. Imagine a heavyweight boxing champion - or an Olympic athlete - coming into your gathering; what will they make of the music? What about that Japanese advertising woman in the back row? Noël Tredinnick, director of music at All Souls always strove for some balance.

'Music should always be servant to the Word,' Noël once told us. 'If it starts to dominate or take people over the top, it is because the inner motivation has ceased to be one of servanthood and love. It is then that it becomes manipulative. But if it is not in your *intention* to manipulate, you won't!

'Take Handel's music,' continued Noël. 'Handel would write out of a love for the Word. He would want his hearers' hearts to soar in tandem with his own; emotions, memories, moods and attitudes would all be involved. The music provides *everybody* – musicians, speaker and hearers alike – with a way of heartfelt response to a magnificent truth.'

On those occasions when music is a part of the proceedings, speakers will be aware of some present who may not share their own Christian beliefs. In presenting the claims of Christ in such a mission context, it seems important and fair not to put words into people's mouths through the thoughtless choice of songs that express ardent spiritual commitment. Items that tell out the truth in an objective way are preferable to those that speak overtly of personal discipleship and adoration.

And singing items should never be banal or sentimental in their terminology. It was Voltaire who said two hundred and fifty years ago, *If a thing is too silly to be said, it can always be sung!*

But enough of the music as such; what of the *speaker* in the evangelistic setting, whose work it is to proclaim Christ and to call for personal response? While not every speaker has an aptitude for this, it seems nevertheless right, at least on occasions, to make the attempt.

What is involved in the putting of such a talk together? The first point is that the evangelist's words should be orientated in a single direction:

One aim in the talk

While this should be the case every time we open our mouths, the importance of the single aim cannot be over-emphasised when, like Aristotle, we are employing 'the art of persuasion' – and with a particular view to summoning our listeners to the feet of Jesus Christ. This is a very ambitious, not to say 'ridiculous' exercise! In the course of a few minutes, we are daring to believe that someone in front of us is going to come to a definite verdict, to share our own faith, to make up their minds about Christ in their lives – in short, to adopt an entirely new world-view!

No wonder the seventeenth century Puritan, Richard Baxter viewed his task with such seriousness:

I preached, as never sure to preach again,

and as a dying man to dying men.

Today's evangelist must be in dead earnest too, with everything about the talk tied carefully into the task in hand.

By that I do not mean for a moment that everything about the address is to give an impression of heavy, other-world 'seriousness' or emotional hype. We should be glad today that we live, for the most part, in the age of the anti-hero. That is a plus in modern evangelistic speaking, because it fits in well with the New Testament approach to proclaiming the news of Christ.

To transfer it to the military metaphor, today's society tends to lean towards England's nineteenth century hero of the Battle of Waterloo, the Duke of Wellington, rather than to more flamboyant commanders of the past. Wellington was the archetypal *anti-hero,* who would avoid high-flown oratory to his troops on the eve of battle, who shrugged away the gold braid, the medals and the acclaim of the masses. Wellington had no time for the calculated gesture, for the rhetoric of Alexander the Great or of his own opponent, Napoleon Bonaparte of France.

To a large degree the television culture has put paid to all that. The power does not lie there, *and it never did*, if we are to understand the apostolic preaching of the Cross properly.

The other side of this is that there is no place for the casual *banter* that reduces Gospel speaking to the telling of the latest 'funnies', interspersed with exhortations to believe. All the greatest evangelists have used humour with telling effect, but not a single one of them could ever remotely have been described as 'a terribly funny speaker'.

The reason is obvious. How can you be funny and trivial, when the centre of your message is the saving death of Jesus Christ who has suffered so that we may escape divine judgment? For the same reason, we shall never meet the person who genuinely repented and came to heaven by way of the Cross, laughing all the way.

Your audience ought to be able to discern that you are in real earnest – from your treatment of the biblical material, your sticking to the theme of the Gospel, and your care in explaining the Cross. You may think that you *know* the message of Christ's death well enough to warrant a mere *Explain the Cross* in your notes; but that is a mistake. *In your notes you should work harder on how God forgives people through Christ's death than on any other part of the talk.* The power to woo and win your listeners to the point of coming to a 'verdict' comes precisely from what Isaac Watts in his hymn called 'the wondrous Cross'.

As you apply this great message to the lives and consciences of those in the audience, your listeners should be able to detect concern and love in your eyes, your voice, your entire attitude. *If these things are there they will show.*

And how to end? Much depends upon the style of the occasion. A well-used approach is to be able to offer a short booklet or pamphlet to those who come up afterwards and ask for one. On certain occasions a 'postscript' talk may be given, for those who stay on as others leave – with a practical explanation of what it means to repent, to count the cost and to receive Christ by his Spirit into our lives.

Be aware that whatever 'ending' is favoured, this is the work of the Spirit of Christ. So I train myself, when inviting people to come up and talk with me at the close, to stand there at the front, relaxed, cheerful and confident that they will come!

In truth it is an awesome prospect – in the power of God *to win your listeners*. Everything should tie in to this, the *one aim in the talk*.

One person in the crowd

To win your listeners, did I say? Better, perhaps, to talk of winning a *listener*. True, you may find yourself at the front of a roomful of people. But all of them are like yourself – a single, fragile bundle of mixed-up emotions and hopes; afloat in a little cockleshell of a very temporary life.

Try and put yourself in the shoes of that one listener. Although you do not, in fact, know precisely to whom you are speaking, nevertheless mentally, spiritually, *it is one person that you are addressing*, no matter how many seats are filled in front of you.

Billy Graham – was he *the* communicator of the twentieth century? – was once being interviewed on television.

'And how many *converts* do you hope to make in this forthcoming event, Dr. Graham?'

'One,' came the reply. 'Just one! If we could make *one* real disciple, it would have been worth coming to your country. If I could win just *you*, it would have been worth coming!'

And that from a man who has spoken to more people face to face than any orator in history. It is a timely reminder of Christ's evaluation of a precious individual, as out-pricing the whole world (Mark 8:36).

Have that one, nameless person in mind as you deliver your message. *There's somebody out there who is being prayed for by a relative, a friend. I don't know who it is, Lord, but You do. Use these words to reach him. May your Spirit touch her!*

An example. There are so many! I select that of Vijay Menon, an engineer in Lloyds Register of Shipping in London. I first met him when he was a patient in Harold Wood Hospital on the borders of London, where I was visiting as a clergyman. From that visit on, he became a member of our church and we became lifelong friends. That very first day I learnt of his experience as a new believer in Jesus Christ.

'For me, it began out of curiosity. You've heard of how curiosity killed the cat? In my case, I was taking a lunch break from my work in the City of London, when I noticed crowds of people turning off the street and entering a large building. Who are these people, and where are they going? I asked myself. I followed them, just to find out!

'When we got inside I looked around me. We were in a religious place! I turned round to retreat, but too late; others were crowding in behind me, and I was trapped. Then I saw the food piled high at the side; I gathered I was in the lunch-hour service of St. Helen's Church in Bishopgate. *If there's food,* I reasoned, *I'll stay.*

'I had entered that place as a devotee of another faith. Forty minutes later I left it as a believer in Jesus Christ! The talk that I heard simply swept away all my prejudices, my antagonisms. I fell in love with Jesus Christ that very day!'

One talk; did the speaker know Vijay was one in the crowd? Did he know that Vijay was to emerge as an outstanding Christian speaker himself, that many thousands would be won to faith in course of time by this Indian layman? That he would serve for many terms in the Church of England's governing body of the General Synod?

Not at all. The speaker had no knowledge of the Asian visitor who left as anonymously as he had arrived.

Later, when Vijay had joined our church, he remarked, '*Somebody* must have been praying for me; in no other way can I explain the transforming power of one talk upon me! But I don't know of anyone who could possibly have been praying for *me*.'

Then one day he found out. It had been his landlady, a shy, retiring Christian woman who had felt too inhibited directly to challenge an overseas male lodger. *But she prayed for Vijay every day.* She then recruited two of her friends to pray as well, even though they had never set eyes upon the Indian engineer. The landlady then died, but the two friends prayed on, every day.

Seven long years passed in all. One day the faithful intercessors opened their *Christian Challenge* newspaper, and on the inside pages saw a large spread, featuring a smiling brown face. It was the story of Vijay Menon! Contact was quickly established, and Vijay had the answer to his puzzle.

A speaker, an intercessor ... and *one person in the crowd*. But there is a third factor to be taken account of, when we are speaking for a verdict:

One link in the chain
Vijay Menon and his intercessors make this point all too clearly. When you stand up to speak, with the intention of explaining the wonderful news of Christ simply enough to help someone make a new start, *you are only a single component in a long process.* Furthermore you have little chance of knowing at *which* point your efforts have contributed.

Is there someone in front of you who has never heard of this before, who represents entirely virgin territory? Is there a member of the audience who has come reluctantly, maybe through the invitation of a friend? Is there yet another listener for whom this could be *the* day of special decision and response?

It is possible to think of an individual's spiritual beginnings in terms of a graph line, numbered from 0 to 100. All along that line there will be a great assortment of incidents, influences, people, books, church sacraments – and talks such as yours. Each has its own part to play; each is a potential link in a chain that is completed when an individual begins to follow Christ in earnest. It is entirely possible that someone listening to your earnest talk on Acts 4:12 is still at only 18 on the graph; so little understood, so much background that needs filling in! Your address may well have its part to play; who knows? Perhaps by the time your message is over, that individual may be at No. 25 on the graph. Be content that this should be so. For on the whole it is unlikely that someone will make the great transition from 0 to 100 in one great step.

For this reason it is a tremendous thing, in student and church settings particularly, to be able to offer members of an audience some kind of a course or study programme that they may take advantage of, as a kind of 'follow-up' to an address of challenge. When enquirers can join such a course, preferably weekly, and in the context of friendship, food and hospitality, *a climate of unhurriedness and space to think is marvellously created.* Numbers of churches in the West experienced a new influx of enquirers, following the confusing events after September 11th 2001 in America - to take one example. We can expect more, as tensions build in our new century. Many of these enquirers have a chequered spiritual background. 'Are you a Christian?' I asked one such. He was from Iraq.

- 'No', he replied. *'But I've been born again'*. It transpired that he had had an encounter with Christ, but had yet to sort out where he stood with his former belief-system. Such a lot to work out! I was glad to speak with him about our own course, *Christianity Explored*, and to refer him to my minister colleague, Rico Tice, its leader. 'It starts with supper!' I said.

Supper, eh? And barbecues? Have you tried your hand at speaking in such surroundings? Even bringing out your old guitar! Bet let's keep these 'specialist' occasions for the next chapter.

*****

And suddenly the shape of a talk has been given me, some half-forgotten incident has flashed into my mind and I was away. Sometimes I had an overwhelming sense that God had some special word for someone present and was using me as his mouthpiece. Later I have found it was so – a thrilling experience, yes, and also awe-inspiring, and in retrospect rather terrifying.

Max Warren, *Crowded Canvas*,
Hodder and Stoughton.

10

EXTEMPORE SPEAKING

Actually, it's a misnomer. My Oxford Dictionary defines extempore speaking as that which is done *without preparation*. On that basis I question whether there is such a thing as public speaking which is carried out without *any* preparation. If there is, it is usually very poor speaking.

'The best spontaneity is invariably rehearsed,' said John Chapman, famed over many years for his apparently effortless campus mission addresses. His statement must not be taken to mean that a talk should be learnt off by heart. That would be to place an intolerable strain on the average speaker, and could well cut the nerve out of speaking that really communicates.

What he meant was that public speaking at its best – including those informal talks that give every appearance of having been pulled out of the air – is the result of material that has been worked over, again and again, in the mind of the speaker. Consequently the sentences are short, the words are mostly of one syllable (as in the case of Churchill), and the language is pictorial. Festo Kivengere of Uganda is now dead, but his challenge to fifteen hundred young people at a meeting I chaired at Keswick in Cumbria still rings in my ears. It was an 'off the cuff' address:

And please don't be shocked when you hear of a revolution in Uganda, a revolution in Burundi, a revolution in Zaire. This is Africa. It's nothing unusual when young countries get revolutions. They are going to get some more! But that does not mean that the Man of Galilee has vacated the Throne. Christianity has never been scared of a revolution. Satan can roar like a lion, but he has no authority to shake the throne on which Jesus is sitting.

'How do these little word pictures and expressions come to you as you speak?' I once asked Festo. 'Are they all written out in your notes beforehand?'

'Usually I get certain ideas written down when I'm preparing,' came the reply, 'and I allow my thoughts to crystallise around them. But I always find *my soul goes beyond my notes in the heat of preaching.*'

Thousands of speakers would testify to the same experience. But now to apply the principles of 'extempore' speaking, to a variety of living situations that are likely to confront you in the course of your speaking career:

At the social
If you are talking in earnest, there are going to be *events* – which will mount up into the hundreds – when you are called upon to give 'a word'. Jazz suppers, bonfire nights, business breakfasts, sports dinners, coffee mornings,

missionary teas, student forums, Christmas parties, barbecues, concerts, annual meetings and book evenings – the chances are that you will do most of these and plenty more!

Some of these will be occasions of Christian outreach; at others you will find yourself surrounded by people you regularly study and pray with. In these latter instances, you will almost invariably choose a sentence, a passage or an idea directly from the Scriptures and have your Bible with you.

What will you take? Perhaps Ephesians 5:14 – the little 'pop song' that found its way into the Bible? Who knows? Perhaps that very song was one of others sung by Paul and Silas in prison (Acts 16:25), during that first momentous trip to Europe:

Wake up, O sleeper;

rise from the dead,

and Christ will shine on you.

Certainly the Philippian jailor was woken up that night! And how about Wesley, centuries later whose own song we still sing: *I woke, the dungeon flamed with light*. And people in the audience before you whom Christ is summoning to *wake up*? To wake up to the Bible, to wake up to prayer, to wake up to the church, to wake up to their own predicament, to wake up to the Cross? Is there a word here in Ephesians 5:14? The Bible is full of these 'words'.

Be building up a storehouse of texts, passages and 'thoughts' that have set your own soul alight, and know where to find them when they are needed.

But what of those other events, when, in a 'neutral' setting, you are invited to speak in a totally informal way about Christian matters, in the presence of many who do not necessarily share your faith? The food has been eaten, the band has stopped playing and everyone has had a very good time. Now you are introduced, to wind up an enjoyable evening. Any advice? Just three pieces:

Be inventive

Think *ahead* to the evening. Anticipate the atmosphere. Work out in advance where you will be standing. Think ahead about your opening gambit. If it is a joke, it needs to be of the kind that doesn't *necessitate* a laugh. How are you going to *fit in*, in a way that really does round off the evening, rather than come as a pill to be swallowed at the end?

And what about notes? How are you going to handle that issue? My favoured way is to have my notes on a very small card in my pocket. Occasionally I peep at the card while the evening progresses. Even while my host is introducing me, I may take a final glance. Then I put the card back in my pocket and leave it firmly there, while I proceed to speak 'extempore'. Once, when I could not quite trust myself to manage without notes, I simply propped them up behind the table flowers. *But I had done a careful reconnoitre of the table layout beforehand.*

Be sensitive

Remember, the guests at this social function have come under the impression that they are going to have a wonderful time! Your closing remarks, then, have got to be in keeping with the style and atmosphere set earlier. It is unlikely that the organisers will have briefed you to be heavy, or overtly judgmental.

But the speaker at these informal events also needs to be sensitive to the *time*. Many are the occasions when, awaiting my turn to speak during an over-packed programme, I have nervously been 'un-preparing' my talk as the minutes have slipped by! People need to get away, and it is not going to help towards the effectiveness of an event if the guests leave, hassled and tired, because the speaker proved unadaptable. Sure, it was not your fault if the programme was over-filled ... but you will have done everyone a good turn if you can edit yourself down, when the occasion demands. I have often marked out the optional cuts in my notes.

Be provocative

You were not invited simply to entertain the guests, but to give them a *focus* as the evening came to a close, perhaps an altogether new and different approach to life? They ought to be thinking as they go off into the night, *That was really something to think about; I hope they'll ask me again to one of those*.

You do not have to be gauche or aggressive to be provocative. It is perfectly possible to slide into your talk enough material to raise *questions* about opposing belief-systems, to *undermine* alternative thought-forms, even to create a little *doubt*!

The reforming British parliamentarian William Wilberforce used to put out what he called 'launchers' during genteel functions two hundred years ago. They would be statements designed to provoke discussion; no harm was done if nobody responded, but a great deal of good resulted if a guest rose to the challenging wit and wisdom of this tireless Christian campaigner. In our own day and culture the same thing can happen again.

Under the spotlight

Put yourself into another context now – the big auditorium, in which you cannot see the audience at all, owing to the dazzling spotlights. As far as I am concerned, such a situation makes it even more important that I have my notes under control. If notes are to be used at all, they should be so familiar to the speaker, and so *legible*, that a single glance is enough to act as a prompt.

Some speakers become intimidated under the hostile lights, a solitary scared, lit-up face squinting anxiously into a black beyond. So train yourself to make *friends* with the lights, to smile wide-eyed into them; how *helpful* of the organisers to light up your talk; and all these great people who have come to this place to have a wonderful time. No, they are not your critics; many of them travelled some way and even paid money for this! True, you can't see them, but they're there all right. Look around you a little. Give them a smile!

On the street

I was in the open air, with a group of my friends. We were about to take turns as soap-box orators, in an attempt to communicate the Christian message. We could hear the comments nearby:

'It's the God-squad. Look at them.'
'O, how nauseating!'

On one thing all are agreed, among those who have taken part in street-preaching. *It is extremely good for the Christians*. This is the real cutting edge of the mission, we say to ourselves, and perhaps we are right. Think of Peter in Jerusalem, Paul in Athens, San Bernardino in Sienna, Whitefield in Georgia and Wesley at Gwennap Pit. Jonathan Edwards, Moody, Palau, Billy Graham – why, among these names you are in honoured company!

The great tip in open-air speaking is, *Do it together*. And *keep* together; don't allow one member of the team to be isolated within a hostile crowd.

You have a penetrating voice? A good pair of lungs? Fine. If you have the use of a microphone, step up to it when it is your turn, keep your mouth about six inches away from it, take a deep breath and *let go*. This is not a cosy, fireside occasion, you are meeting the great public in the raw.

Although it is good to brandish a Bible, the open-air speaker is not advised to embark on detailed and erudite Bible expositions. They will get lost in the wind, the traffic, the police sirens! *It is Bible text and slogan time when you're on the soap box*. Speakers at other open-air events, and great stadium rallies of Christian witness, are in agreement. Keep the sentences short and crisp. Keep the talk moving along. The moment one speaker steps down, another should get up. Time is limited, attention is easily distracted and people will be coming and going continuously. If they can catch *one sentence* of value, the operation will have been worth while.

And hecklers? You have to live by your wits! One recommendation, however, is that if a disturbance is caused, *do not immediately look in its direction, not even momentarily.* Keep talking over the top; you need to buy yourself a little time while you think out your next move – whether to respond verbally or keep going. And, as a matter of fact, this is a good strategy for *any* meeting in which you are the speaker. On numbers of occasions, I have chosen not to notice the disturber of the peace (who may well be drunk). Colleagues can sort out the problem while the talk goes on!

Street drama, sketch boards, music – and plenty of literature; all these are valuable parts of the exercise. And people *will* be helped. On more than one occasion, a visitor at our church Newcomers' Night will tell me, 'I've come because of some people I met from your church. They were speaking in Leicester Square.'

In the studio

The *radio* talk ... hardly 'extempore'. No, it is not extempore at all, but it has got to *sound* extempore. If you are called upon to give a 'Thought for the Day' on radio, your contribution has to come across as pacey, animated chatter. You may find yourself slotted in between the news bulletin and the weather forecast.

Anticipation then, is one of the necessary arts of the radio broadcaster. What is the *style* of this radio station, and of this particular programme? What time of day will it be for the listeners? Will they be at breakfast, in bed, driving the car? What will be occupying their minds as you go out on air? What are the current public issues? What is happening in the world just now? All these are important factors that will shape the writing of your script.

Admittedly you cannot anticipate everything. During the Gulf War of 1991, I went out live on air over the BBC, three mornings in a row. On the third morning, February 28th, I was rung by my producer at the crack of dawn.

'Richard? Christine here. Look, it's all changed during the night. The war's *over*!'

'Over? Oh my. Okay, there's just time; I'll rewrite the script.'

And that is what I had to do, breathlessly, in my pyjamas, before flinging on some clothes and hurrying over to Broadcasting House.

A little nerve-racking? Yes, but it's exciting too. Part of the fascination lies in your ignorance of the audience. How many people are out there listening? Don't let the audience-figures sap your determination that you are going to speak to *one person*. As with the spotlight, make friends with the microphone! But now you are not speaking in a large hall; you are talking, at conversational level – and at conversational speed to a single individual. The radio audience has no right of reply, so you are not going to be 'preach-ey'. But you are not there to be flabby either! If you are going to give something in the nature of a *Thought for the Day*, the aim is that you will give the listener something from God's self-revelation that will stay in the mind throughout the entire *day*. A really well done 'Thought' *can* last a lifetime!

You write or type your script on one side of the paper only, *sliding* the top copy across the table as you move on to the next sheet. And you are wise not to type the script right down to the bottom of the paper – for, as your eyes follow the type down the page, so your mouth will imperceptibly distance itself from the microphone, and that could affect sound quality.

Learn, if you have not already done so, to speak a strange language; it is called *Internationalese*. After all, who is listening to you on that radio set? Why, you have Hispanics, Afro-Caribbeans and Chinese as part of your audience. Some of them may understand only half your talk. While doing justice to your own host culture, set a limit on those idioms, historical allusions and literary quotations that only a proportion of your listeners can understand. The apostle Paul surely knew all about this.

Radio ... And last of all?

Telling your story
The *testimony*, as it has often been called; how you began as a Christian, how you got going! For many Christians, the testimony was their first experience of public speaking. How do you go about it?

First, it is a testimony to a Person and what he has done for you.

You are not asked to be on your feet to pay tribute to a book, a Christian, a course or a church that may have helped you, though any of these may legitimately come into the story. But it is *Jesus Christ*, and what he has so far done for you that you are wanting to focus upon primarily.

Second, it is a testimony and not a mini-sermon that you are giving.

Three and a half minutes is enough - unless you have been invited to speak for longer. The whole style is that of telling a story. It is unwise, then, to attempt to do the *preacher's* task. Use a text, by all means, if there is something from the Scriptures that has meant a great deal in your spiritual beginnings. But don't end the testimony by a long exhortation to commitment; that is almost certainly someone else's job in the proceedings.

Third, it is a testimony and not an essay.
Although it may well be wise to write out, word for word, what you intend to say (this can help you to keep to time), have your notes on a small jotting pad or card, rather than on a large, distracting sheet of paper. The whole presentation is essentially one of spontaneity and an impulsive *desire to tell*. Write it out as you would describe it to your best friend in the chair opposite you.

You may want to follow some simple format; for example: 1. *Before.* 2. *What happened.* 3. *The difference Christ makes now.* There is no need to be apologetic, and no reason to feel intimidated. Your story and experience are unique!

Years ago my mother, on returning to Britain after a period of Christian work in Kenya, was asked to speak about life, lived among the Kikuyu people, at a meeting of anthropologists. As she told the family later, 'I was completely terrified when I arrived at the hall. They all seemed to be professors, and very learned at that. It was only just before I got up to speak, that God put the reassurance into my mind, *"None of these men have ever been in a Kikuyu house."* The knees immediately stopped shaking.'

This is your reassurance too. Your story is a one-off! There has not been, and never will be again, anybody like you in the whole history of the world. Your story is unparalleled to anybody else's. God never repeats his wonders! Whether your story is uncomplicated or dramatic, it is a story that will never be told by anybody else.

So speak it out boldly, and speak *up*! You see that man at the very back? He looks half asleep. Just lean into those words a bit and see if you can wake him up. No need to gabble out the words. Take your time over it; this is a story of God and yourself. But can it be told in three and a half minutes? It can if you write it out first. Even then allowance has to be made for the slowing down that the acoustics of an auditorium can cause. *You will be amazed*.

It is not at all too pretentious to ask in prayer that some in the audience will be touched by your words, to the extent that they, in their own turn, will be tipped into the Kingdom of God. It is very much the way it has happened from the beginning. *One loving spirit sets another on fire*, explained Augustine of Hippo, back in the fourth century AD. Ask that *one* will be 'set on fire', through your words.

And in all this 'extempore' speaking, rehearsed, worked through and delivered - to God be all the credit. Nothing can happen without the power of his Spirit.

*****

PART THREE

* * * * *

HOW TO PROGRESS

For me, this will be heaven. I love serving God. And if we've been faithful in earthly service, our responsibility in heaven will increase proportionately. No, I take that back. It won't be increased in proportion. God's too generous for that. Our service will increase completely out of proportion. It doesn't take a rocket scientist to read the formula Jesus gives in His heaven parable in Luke 19:17: '"Well done, my good servant!" his master replied. "Because you have been trustworthy in a very small matter, take charge of ten cities."'

Joni Eareckson Tada,
Heaven ... Your Real Home, Zondervan.

Gracious God, remember us in our work this day. May we turn nothing out half done. May we glorify thee by honest good work; for the sake of him who completed his work for us, even Jesus Christ our Lord. Amen.

J.H. Jowett, 1911.

11

PUTTING THE TALK TO BED

The de-briefing – how important! It could even be argued that the main work of a talk begins *after* it has been delivered. Go to the back of any fair-sized auditorium after a guest speaker has come and gone, and look around. Why, the place is like a beehive.

There's a gang of people dismantling the platform set-up. Microphones and P.A. are being stowed away. The bookstall is coming into its own at this point. So is the refreshment counter. Conversations are starting up around the hall. You couldn't tell, just to look at it – but *spiritual* links are being forged before your eyes:

'It was my first time here; how often do you meet?'

'In the announcements I heard something about a course you were starting here. Could you put my name down for that?'

'Glad you could come; what did you think of the talk?'

'I've just arrived from Pittsburgh; do you have a Bible study I could join?'

Later on still, someone will come in to clean the room which only hours earlier was buzzing with activity. The people have gone, and the work that went into that speaking function is now evidently over.

But it's not over. As the last person left the building, do we really imagine for a moment that God – if we may put it reverently – dusted his hands and said, 'Well, that's that'? Not if we take the Scriptures seriously. Jesus, when criticised for heal-ing on the Sabbath day, made the point that *God's* work never stops:

> My Father is always at his work to this very day, and I, too, am working (John 5:17).

The merely negative view of the Sabbath as a day of inaction and rest *from* human labour, was to give way to that of a day of rest *for* divine activity and loving service. We're caught up in this.

The work of God continues long after the talk is given. It is, after all *his* work that we have been a part of. If he is continuing his work in the lives of people that we have been addressing in his Name, then we must believe that he is working within *us*, too, his servants.

> What did this experience of service do for *us*?
>
> What have we learnt, that we hadn't learnt before?
>
> How can we absorb for ourselves the same truths that we have been teaching others?
>
> How can we be more effective for the next time?

There is much more to finishing a speaking engagement than throwing the notes into a drawer and switching on the television. Involved in putting the talk to bed there is a fair amount of work to be done. How shall we identify it?

Putting the Talk to Bed

Review the contents

Garth Hewitt and I were on a tour of Uganda. He was the singer and I was the speaker. We were representing African Enterprise, at the invitation of the Church of Uganda, and we did thirty concerts in ten days. There was barely time to 'review' at all with such a hectic schedule.

The audiences themselves were a barometer as to how things were going.

'You can probably drop your fifth song,' I said to Garth early in the tour.

'*Big Black Mamba*? You're right; it only got a patter of applause. Why was that, do you think?'

'It must be the fact that we don't have snakes like that in the UK; *we* can find them morbidly fascinating. But here in Africa, black mambas are just part of the local fauna and flora!'

But then I, as the speaker, needed all the briefing – and de-briefing – that *I* could get. In my case, it was our Ugandan driver who provided the tips.

'Richard, please include that story of the English butler from now on!'

'O, okay, John. But why?'

'Well, you see, it opens up to us something about your past English culture. Everyone was hooked by your story. And then you gave it that twist at the end!'

It was the driver who, again early in the tour, decided that I hadn't been quite direct enough in the talk to students. As I stopped, he marched up to the front and took over the microphone:

'And those of you who want to make your decision for Christ, come forward *now*!'

Speaking in Public - Effectively

The local man knows best, I reflected, as young people - to my amazement - made their way forward. Forget the visiting clergyman. Leave it to the driver!

Review, review, review. Unless we do that, we can never grow. How did the talk go? Why did people start shuffling towards the end? What ought to have been *omitted*? Did the talk make one great Scriptural point, or did secondary material creep in? It was the great Swiss theologian Karl Barth who emphasised this issue in his comments about preaching:

> Once the preacher wants his sermon to fulfil a second function over and above the service of the divine word, and plans it that way, this second function wins the day and the preaching ceases to serve the word
>
> *(Karl Barth,* Eberhard Busch, Fortress Press).

Look again at your notes, now that the talk is done. Don't put them away just yet! Was there a main point and aim that came across? Or was the message in reality a stringing together of several separate messages? Was there enough in the talk to make listeners stop and think? Or was the evening not much more than a great time? We would certainly want an occasion for Christ to be 'a great time', but we must remember that *it is impossible to pass on a great time to the next generation.*

D.L. Moody of old may not have got his grammar and syntax perfected. Indeed in the last letter he ever wrote, there were thirty-six spelling mistakes. But in his public speaking he never failed to make his point. Of him, a learned Chicago theological professor wrote:

Putting the Talk to Bed

It is perfectly astounding to me that a man with so little training should have come to understand the public so well. He cannot read the Greek Testament; indeed he has difficulty with parts of it in the *English* version, but he excels any man I have ever heard in making his hearers see the point of a text of Scripture

(*Moody without Sankey*, J.C. Pollock, Christian Focus).

The English seventh Earl of Shaftesbury compared Moody at that time with the greatest Tractarian preacher of the day, Canon Liddon, and wrote, 'Moody will do more in an hour than Canon Liddon in a century'.

Go over that talk again. If necessary, go over it with a friend. If it was recorded, listen to the tape, watch the video, for faithful are the wounds of the tape machine! *Review the contents.*

Record the details

This is an important part of putting the talk to bed. It is the long term approach to public speaking. For that reason I no longer grudge the time that I spend putting to rest a talk on which I earlier spent several hours of preparation. If, I reason to myself, it was worth putting in the early study, groundwork and sheer discipline in excavating the right words to convey God's message, then let me not lose the fruit of this labour by carelessness at the end:

What Scripture passage did this talk relate to?
What main topic or topics did it cover?
When did I give this address?
Where did I give this address?

How long did I speak for?

What illustrations, stories and quotations did I use?

Where precisely will I find the notes of this talk again?

Have I catalogued for future use any *new* stories or illustrations that I used?

What were the main headings of my message, so that I may make a note of them at the edge of the page in my wide-margin Bible?

Most of these details can be attended to, either with the use of a computer or, as in my case, with the help of the card-index systems. I find it to be creative, satisfying and therapeutic work. It can sometimes take me as much as an hour to carry out this exercise. Its valuable by-product is that it provides a further way of absorbing the message into my own soul. On occasions I find myself able to improve upon my talk; at times changing a heading and editing out of the notes items that, on looking back, I felt had not helped the main argument.

For one day I will come back to this message and have another run at it. By the grace of God it will be better next time! All the more reason, then, that I should not have to waste unnecessary time in trying to trace my notes. They have been safely put to bed. My last task is to give the right hand margins of all the cards their own distinguishing colour, for easy later identification in the card index.

And the wide-margin Bible, with the outlines of every Bible talk I have ever given? *That is my back-up system*. From the beginning it seemed to me that if I was in for a lifetime of this speaking, it would be wise to have a second record of at least the bones of my addresses, kept separately. The additional bonus is that, when undecided about the subject of an impending address, I have found it stimulating to be able to turn the pages of my wide-margin Bible and prayerfully ruminate. Sometimes an old outline will leap out at me and claim a re-run.

My battered wide-margin Bible is, what the saints of old used to call, *much-used*. I had to have it rebound at one time. On many pages there has not been enough room to include further outlines. I have then had to resort to white 'Tipp-Ex', in my decision to obliterate an earlier outline that I had now grown beyond. If archaeologists ever unearth my wide-margin Bible in future ages, they will doubtless be able to penetrate to the outlines of those first messages, and will authoritatively pronounce my manuscript to be what is technically called a *palimpsest!*

It is important to emphasise that we should not use a marked Bible like this for regular Bible *study*; we need to come to the word of God freshly, without having our understanding coloured and even clouded by extraneous human material.

Recording the details. Whatever the precise system used, the benefit of taking care over these matters may well prove incalculable in future years. If you have a mind to do it, *begin at once*. There is no time to lose.

There is a third priority that every public speaker needs to attend to, when the address is over.

Receive the comments

We were busy making scrambled egg for the visiting Americans. They were seated at the table in our living room, drinking fresh orange juice, as they discussed the day's play at the Wimbledon tennis. The player ... and the coach – it was a privilege for us to give them accommodation in London during the greatest two weeks of the year for international tennis.

I kept well out of the conversation as I brought them their scrambled egg, for I knew that a de-briefing was going on.

'Remember?' said the coach, 'you had him at 3-2 and thirty-love. That was the critical point of the whole set! If you hadn't goofed that easy volley you'd have been forty-love up, and the game would almost certainly have been yours. You'd then have been 4-2 up, with the set looking *good*. As it was, you let him back in, and let me remind you that 3-3 is very different from 4-2. You'd have saved yourself an awful lot of hard work if you'd just *thought* when you were at thirty-love!'

As we put the coffee on, I reflected. *A coach is your fiercest critic, but is also your best friend.* Naturally the coach wants you to do well, to *win*. This simple fact alone guarantees that you will be pushed, even goaded, into working harder for the next time.

We who are public speakers should apply this lesson to our own field. There will certainly be *friends*, who will give us words of encouragement:

'Hey, that was great. I found it such a help.'
'That was marvellous. I loved it.'
'You were on good form. It was wonderful.'

It is in the cold light of the following day that we could do with a friend who is also our *critic* – and who, if possible, knows something about it. These people are not always easy to find. Sometimes they will be diffident about analysing your talk – for two reasons.

First, they are all too aware of their own weaknesses and bad speaking habits. Secondly, they may well be nervous of interfering with your own unique gift, and of turning you into someone you ought not to be. But if you push them, they will be able to spot some of the faults, the imbalances of a talk, the strange eccentricities that can distract the audience.

It was a well-known English politician about whom journalists, arriving late for the rally, would ask, 'Has he done the light bulb yet?' It was noticeable that at a certain point of any speech, the orator's hand would reach up, curl and *twist*. The gesture could only be likened to changing an electric light bulb. Once this mannerism had been noticed and remarked upon, it could only take away from the impact of the speaking. Irreverent members of the audience then begin to make a *count* of these little tricks and habits. Find a trustworthy coach who knows what needs to be ironed out and what does not!

The best guides are those who will listen to you several times before venturing to make constructive criticisms. On the other side, the better *speakers* will prove to be those with the humility to listen to themselves on tape, and to ask and receive advice from the more experienced.

When, in the future, you find yourself bedding down a talk, murmur to yourself, *There is always a next time*.

*****

Mother, pay the man and let us go home.

J.G. Simpson, *Preachers*.

12

WILL THEY INVITE YOU AGAIN?

I hate to see an empty seat. There are the optimists and the pessimists in this regard, and each of these categories found an exemplar in my two parents. My father was the optimist. In my youth, I would watch him as he put out the chairs at home for a meeting. He would cram as many chairs into the room as possible – the rows tightly compacted, the seats all touching.

My mother would then walk round the arrangements behind him, reducing the rows and widening the spaces. She was the pessimist. To her way of thinking it would be a marvel if anyone turned up.

'Eke them out,' she would murmur, as she quietly stacked chairs away again. 'They must still *look* as many as possible, because we want a full room. And if extra people do arrive, it'll be a nice surprise for everyone to hear the call, *More chairs needed please*!'

There is something about *fullness* that provides added value to a public event. I was once asked to speak in a large hall that had been booked for a special evening event. I was dumbfounded on arrival to discover that the organisation had unaccountably omitted to put out any publicity at all. Even the chief organiser failed to arrive until five minutes before the start, and then only to tender apologies that he was not, after all, able to stay for the duration. I was left gazing at five hundred seats, a row of spotlights *and twelve members of the public*. Miraculously they had defied the publicity bloc, and had managed to discover the venue.

My morale was not lifted when, at the end, an elderly man waited to speak with me under the lamplight outside. He surveyed me kindly, hands on hips.

'Well,' he smiled, '*Sorry you couldn't fill it*.' He paused, then added, 'Never mind; Billy Graham started small.' I left for home.

Most speakers will, at some point, share an experience I had, of arriving for a youth organisation's Birthday meeting, to be confronted by an audience of *one*. It was difficult to know where to look when, after a full programme of songs, prayers and even notices, I was invited to stand up and deliver my prepared Birthday Message.

But horror stories have an unfortunate way of working both ways. I tingle with shame when I think of speaking engagements that I have messed up or even double-booked. There must, for a variety of reasons, be certain organisations and groups who have black-listed me for ever! It is to save speaking colleagues causing unnecessary distress and offence that this chapter is written.

How will your address be remembered?
Having heard you once, would the organisers wish to invite you back a second time? Imagine that you have just fulfilled a speaking engagement for a body previously

unknown to you. Now, knowing your own weaknesses and strengths, ask yourself the following five questions. All of them interrelate, and even overlap a little. But all are relevant.

Did you enrich them or did you short-change them?

That is to say, did you give the audience basically what your hosts had asked for? There has to be a degree of mutual trust in putting on a meeting with an address. For their part, the organisers had been given to understand that you were a speaker worth having in their programme. They took a risk in inviting you! On your side, you believed that the committee acted responsibly in devising this particular series in which you participated.

The temptation sometimes for a busy speaker is to try and get away with an old talk which is at least *close* to the required topic. But does this build trust for the next time?

Alternatively, an old talk may be brought out, which is right on the target, *but which needed to be overhauled completely before delivery*. The speaker hopes that the lack of preparation will be undetected, and indeed, may persist in this habit of skimping the hard work, *unaware that a reputation is slowly building up for a slapdash approach to speaking*. The speaker may remain blissfully ignorant of this reputation, for it is a brave organiser who takes the visitor to task when the meeting is over. I myself have chaired meetings, and noticed, from behind, the shuffling of jumbled notes, sometimes tattered and even yellowing with age; the rapid flipping over of pages that the speaker has decided to discard – and have thought to myself, *This has all the hallmarks of a very tired talk*. As often as not the speaker will then complain that there was not enough *time*!

That is to short-change an audience. To be invited to speak is an honour, and it is very important that both organisers and audience feel at the end that they have been given full measure, the best of which the speaker was capable, fresh, up-to-date, and coming right out of their present-day walk with God.

Here now to tax us is a second question, allied to the first:

Did you respect them or did you despise them?

The moment we sense that we are a cut above our audience – that the message we have prepared will 'do' for them – we should pull ourselves up short and repent of a patronising tendency that smacks of contempt.

Actually if you genuinely love people you will not fall into this attitude. Many are the ministers and servants of God who have come to the realisation that they did *not* love others. Yet their testimony has been that as, in heartfelt prayer, they persistently asked the Lord to give them a love for people, God did this very thing for them.

Love is indispensable. We cannot touch people – their heartfelt decisions, loyalties and affections – with the message of God in a life-changing way, without this virtue. If we don't love people we can only come across, at best, as sterile preaching machines.

Such speakers arrive at the meeting wrapped up in themselves. They find it impossible to 'enjoy' the rest of the meeting because they are caught up in their own preoccupations. They fail to engage or socialise with the audience at the end, because they are living unto themselves. All too often, because they cannot respect the wishes of the organisers, they will ask at short notice whether they can change the title they have been given. I have heard this done even as they stand up to speak.

'The Lord has told me to change from the announced subject. Instead I am going to give you my testimony.'

The last time I heard this done, I was not impressed by the lacklustre talk that followed. True, there *are* moments when God so lays hold of a speaker that they have no option but to alter course. But in general, to do this in the face of a publicised topic or passage is to undermine the wisdom of the organisers in choosing the subject in the first place. *In my own experience the resulting talk is usually a let-down.*

Trust that God answered the prayers of the group who selected *you* to deliver the desired talk! Don't gain a reputation for ignoring the chair, ignoring the brief and ignoring the clock. Those with such a reputation are not quickly asked back.

A third question – and again it is linked to the other two:

Did you up-build them or did you exploit them?

An audience that you have just left should feel that it has *gained* from your visit. You may indeed have challenged the members deeply, but it will have been done with a view to establishing them more firmly – to the point, even, that in years to come some will retain a lasting sense of indebtedness for a memorable talk.

So our third question is not concerned about whether the address left people feeling cosy or comfortable. It is rather asking *how trustworthy you are, as a speaker, to be let loose on an audience.* Those who invited you have already displayed trust – great trust – in bringing you to a fellowship that no doubt they have been steadily building up for years.

We dare not betray that trust. Many are the meetings that suffer from hijackers, who spring unwanted surprises on the event, who put the organisers on the spot – publicly – with questions designed to show up their lack of knowledge, to embarrass or humiliate. Such practitioners, with no previous knowledge of the personnel present, will have little compunction about singling out individual members of the audience for public attention or comment, thus effectively ensuring (especially if those members are newcomers) that they will never return. The organisers are then left to pick up the pieces. Let any who have behaved in this conceited and opinionated way check on the number of times they have been invited back to the gathering they visited.

The issue has nothing to do with polite, public school 'nice' behaviour. It has everything to do with the Christian virtue of *grace*. Stephen the martyr was scathingly bold when he spoke of the sins that had led to the death of his master, Jesus, but his speaking still represented a combination of 'grace and power' (Acts 6:8).

We may console ourselves as speakers that we have never behaved in an insensitive, gross manner – but it is as well to check. Do you – however unconsciously – take out your frustrations, after a difficult journey, on the audience? If the lighting in the room is bad, do you feel obliged to comment on it? Or the quality of the public address system? That badly-chosen song ... the inept title you were given to speak on?

Will They Invite You Again?

Your public criticisms, as the invited guest, will be taken as a reflection on the organisers; is that what you intended? You may even suspect inwardly that you were only invited in the first place to be a 'programme-filler', but it must be remembered that you accepted the invitation to speak not for 'them' primarily, but for *Him*. You are Christ's representative in that place. And the audience in front of you is composed of people just like yourself – a bundle of sins, prejudices and habits. Christ died for them as much as he died for you, *and the ground is level at the Cross*. No Christian speaker who has been *there* will ever use or exploit the flock of Christ.

Three check questions. Now here is a fourth:

Did you inform them or did you confuse them?
Imagine a boatload of people. They are setting off from the mainland, and their planned destination is an island, straight ahead. It is island A. About five degrees to the right is another island, B. Then, at ninety degrees to the left there is a third island, C. Inside the boat an argument is going on.

'That's the island we want. Can't you see it, right ahead? Check it with the map, Island A.'

'You're wrong! Make a ninety-degree turn at once, over to Island C on the left. We're way off course!'

'No, no; I've got an instinct for direction. It's B we want, just marginally to the right. Alter course by a fraction!'

Question: *Who is the most dangerous guide in the boat?*

The quick answer would identify the advocate for Island C. Why, if the passengers follow this advice they are going to be irreparably off course. But a little thought persuades us otherwise. For C is so *obviously* the wrong island that none but the very dimmest are going to be taken in by such patently bad advice.

No, it is the enthusiast with an instinct for Island B who represents the real danger. The unwary, the waverers, could very easily be deceived by directions that are so close to the true. So close – and look friends, Island B looks rather more exciting than Island A in any case! Take an inspired risk; *go for it*.

True, if the option is for Island B, the boatload of people will only *just* lose the way, *but it will be lost just the same.*

That is the frightening, the really frightening, factor about giving direction to others through the spoken message. My advice is, 'Stay frightened!' How do you wreck a church, a fellowship? Just join the band of truth-warpers who sow seeds of division and confusion in households and whole communities. Ninety-five percent of what they teach sounds plausible, even orthodox. It is the *slant* they adopt, the five percent angle of error that does the damage.

The vital standard of biblical *soundness* is often treated as a joke in today's cynical world, even among Christian people.

'Do they think I'm *sound* enough?' some will ask with wry amusement.

When people put that question to me, I take it as a sure-fire indication of a troubled conscience. Almost certainly they are not sound enough to be trusted with a roomful of listeners with open Bibles in front of them. Then, naturally, I must ask myself, *Am I sound enough?* For our brief is to do with what the Bible writers call 'the faith that was once for all entrusted to the saints' (Jude 3), 'the pattern of sound teaching', the 'good deposit that was entrusted to you' (2 Tim. 1:13, 14), 'the trustworthy message', and 'sound doctrine' (Titus 1:9).

Deviate from it, warns Jude, the earthly brother of Jesus Christ, and you will become as unproductive as clouds without rain, or autumn fruit trees without fruit. You may end up even like a spectacular shooting star, ascending high into the ecclesiastical firmament and capturing the Christian headlines for a while, but descending again into the darkest night (Jude 12, 13).

That, then, is the question; did you stick to the truth of the Bible? Did you inform your listeners in its truths, or did you leave them off course and confused?

Let us be content ourselves with a last check question for the aspiring speaker:

Did you refresh them or did you exhaust them?
Make life as easy as possible for your hosts! You are *not* the celebrity guest who needs the red carpet treatment; you are a servant of the Lord Jesus Christ. You've come, in the grace and power of God to provide a *lift* for everybody. So keep your demands down to the minimum. If you are even a little swollen with your own self-importance, you are likely to be creating waves around yourself!

'Great to be with you, but do you have a phone here that I can use? Oh and a photocopier please.'

'I'm afraid I can't speak without a lectern; you didn't tell me there wouldn't be one.'

'I wonder if it would be all right to have three or four helpers offering these leaflets at the door as people leave? They're for a special event I'm involved with.'

It doesn't take much; a few demands, a bit of fuss ... and presently an unspoken thought will surface in your hosts' minds: *The next time, forget it; it would have been easier to do this ourselves.*

As a matter of fact, it is nearly always more draining to have a visiting speaker than to organise the event in-house. Part of the reason is that you know your own people, their needs and capacities – and you may find yourself, as organiser, on the edge of your seat with a certain nervous tension as the address progresses, wanting the speaker to fulfil expectations, to hold the attention, to deliver the goods, to stop on time!

If you, then, *are* the visiting speaker, be aware of your hosts' concerns, so that they are left at the close, not so much relieved at your departure, as refreshed by the inspiration of your self-giving, and by the message that you brought.

And the small matter of 'expenses'? Let's save that for part of chapter 15!

*****

When it is only the style of the speaking that is remembered, the Cross is likely to be emptied of its power.

R. C. Lucas,
Proclamation Trust, 1991.

13

THINGS THAT BLUNT THE TALK

'There's a wonderful life in front of us, if only we will have it! It won't be God's fault if we miss it. And it won't be *my* fault, because I'm telling you now!'

There was no microphone for the speaker out there on London's Tower Hill, but the words would be heard above the traffic for a quarter of a mile in each direction. It was Steve Rowe, one of our London open-air speakers, who was giving it his all as he spoke from Luke 16, on the theme of the Rich Man and Lazarus.

As he once explained to me, 'When I became a Christian, I used to hear people enthusing about Spurgeon, Whitefield and Wesley and their wonderful speaking. I would reply, I'd like to go and hear them.'

'Oh, you can't do that!'

'Well, could you give me their phone numbers then?'

'It was then explained to me that these people had been dead for years,' said Steve. 'And I thought to myself, *If they are dead now, who's getting up to speak in their place?*

'And that,' declared Steve, 'is how I came to start public open-air speaking. The Lord gives us today what he gave us in the past!'

Speaking in Public - Effectively

On that August day, at the recognised speaker's spot near the Tower of London, hundreds of people were stopped dead in their tracks as the voice boomed out. No shouting was necessary. Passers-by on Tower Bridge 300 yards away leaned out over the Thames to listen to the words as they ricochetted off walls and roofs. Residents leaned out of the nearby block of flats; others stood on balconies. People came out of the nearby McDonalds' restaurant to gape. Japanese tourists delayed getting into their coaches, despite their driver's impatience, wanting to hear Steve finish his half-hour address.

Yes, it really is for today. If laymen like Steve can pick up the torch, so can you. You may not necessarily have the projection that can span the Thames, but in all likelihood you have a gift, or you would not be reading this book. How to *build* on the gift? How to iron out the kinks and hindrances that can get in the way of effective speaking? There is more to it than getting the exposition right in Luke 16 and then (however prayerfully) enunciating the words you have prepared. Let those who think that is *all there is to it*, try it out and see if they can win a regular hearing!

The contention of this chapter is that God uses hard work. First we must get the content right. Unless we can give prime care to this, we would be better not to start at all. It takes a very great deal of work just to get the message straight, the Scripture *right*!

Then, all along the line, we need to put in extra work on those elements in our speaking that *hinder* the word we have been given from being properly heard and received. Are *we* somehow in the way? It takes work and persistence to rid ourselves of those things that block our communication. To begin with, across the tradition of Christian speaking there has always been a problem over *time*.

Excessive length

It is partly nervousness that makes some speakers fill out the talk unnecessarily; nervousness that they will not be able to produce a 'substantial' address or exposition, worthy of the name. This hits us at virtually every level of public speaking. If someone has been briefed to fill a four-minute information slot in the prayer gathering, it is no great surprise if they end up taking eight. It is because we feel somehow that we must justify our presence there in front of a lot of people.

Most modern speakers vastly overestimate the listening capacity of their audience. It is not for me to dictate how long an address should last. Frankly, most of us are just not good enough to sustain more than twenty-five minutes. The majority of talks and sermons could be edited down by a fifth, without losing too much. The only speaker I have ever known whose talks were impossible to edit down without causing damage was John Stott.

The seventeenth century French reformed minister Jean Claude, in his famous *Essay on the Composition of a Sermon*, condemned what he called 'dry and barren explications' as 'extremely disgustful':

'A sermon *cold* and *poor*,' he wrote, 'will do more mischief in an hour, than a hundred rich sermons can do good.'

Surely the moral for us is, *Do not read protracted Scripture essays aloud till the end of time, and imagine that you have been engaged in public speaking.*

Some further 'blunting' aspects we should be aware of:

Clichés, slang and Latin

Around us every day there are phrases and sayings that are boringly familiar; we use them without thought; they simply add clutter to our public speaking, and make it yawningly predictable and platitudinous. Worse, in front of international people, they can positively obscure our meaning. In our own United Kingdom, here are a few such clichés that have gone the rounds in recent years:

> *I was gutted.*
> *The best thing since sliced bread.*
> *When all's said and done.*
> *A truly mind-blowing experience.*
> *Now this is the bottom line.*
> *I was absolutely gobsmacked.*
> *Been there, done that, got the T-shirt.*
> *At the end of the day.*

It does not make for good communication when the audience could finish off the sentence for you; for example, 'We ignore prayer ... at our peril.' The *slang* phrases are best eased out of the talk. A preaching colleague of mine once used the sentence, *Peter was in danger of losing his bottle.* It was a German member of the congregation who came up puzzled at the end.

'This bottle of Peter I cannot find in the passage,' he insisted. 'What was in the bottle?'

Things that Blunt the Talk

We should also be chary of the overdone words of the modern media: 'Tragically', 'arguably', 'hopefully', 'sadly', 'incredibly'.

And why are Latin terms thought to be more sophisticated, a little *grander* than Anglo Saxon? They actually blunt our communication. Knock out of your script such words as *commence*, *prior to*, and *sufficient* – and replace them with *start* or *begin*, *before* and *enough*. It will make a difference.

Unnecessary jargon

I refer now to the slipshod phrases that litter modern speaking, often through sheer laziness. Words like *just* and phrases such as *If you like* and *In other words* are everywhere! A couple of rhetorical questions may be admissable but - in a single talk – to hear twenty and more of *arn't we?....isn't it?....don't they?....haven't we?* is a result of the inbred school of tapes and conferences that feed much of our work today. They blunt the force of our speaking, and add to the tedium. This is how we can sound:

I think what I am trying to say is this: As our church comes under the searchlight of Christ's gaze – *so to speak* – we *just* need to be asking ourselves one big question, *don't we*? Have we forsaken our first love? That's the question we should be asking at the *commencement* of a new millennium, *isn't it*? We want, *as it were*, to ensure that our light – our lamp-stand, *if you like* – is never removed from this town. *In other words*, Christ is calling on us to repent and do those first works, *isn't he*? I hope that *each and every one of us* will take Revelation 2 to heart. It's a challenging passage, *isn't it*? Look at verse 7. *As I say* ...

Apply yourself to these phrases, and work on them. I find it difficult to believe that any speaker would *plan* to include such useless verbiage. Was it there in the scripted draft? Almost certainly not! But it gets into the final product. If you don't believe me, listen to a tape of your last talk and check. If you are guilty of using a particular piece of blunting terminology, *do an actual count through the talk*; you could be amazed. It is very unlikely that a friend will do this for us; we will have to spot these habits for ourselves, and it takes work. But the end result will be a keener, sharper instrument for the Word.

Cut out those 'in-house' terms that subtly exclude the enquiring visitor:

As Henry said in his talk last week.... Now, before I hand you over to Kate ....
(Henry who? Kate who?)
Let me just say to you in CYFA .... It's a joy to us all that Christine is going out with Y-Wam ....

(CYFA? That means nothing. And who is this guy Y-Wam? A member of the church staff perhaps?)
Terminology ... but now illustrations that blunt.
But can any illustration hurt a talk?

Inept illustrations
'Lord, give me a talk for this fabulous illustration.' How many of God's servants have prayed in this way! Of course,

there is nothing like the perfect illustration or story to break open an eternal truth. Jesus, the greatest storyteller in the history of the world, knew the power of the right story for the right truth.

We do not always. Too often, in our eagerness for illustrations, we are like squirrels looking for nuts, and when we find one, we long to put it to immediate use. But it truly may not *fit*. There are some stories permanently looking for a talk. Let them wait, however great the temptation to blow them. The wrong story, an inept joke, can well destroy the talk's main theme.

Some illustrations are altogether too interesting and fascinating in themselves, and can *divert* the audience from the message. There are stories that should never be told.

Sometimes a story is narrated as the personal experience of the speaker, when it was not. It is beyond me to understand how a Christian speaker could even be *tempted* in this direction. But it happens. The sense of let-down is enormous when the real truth is discovered (and it will be discovered one day). A congregation or fellowship *may* smile when it transpires that, after all, the event described never took place, *but something of trust will die that day*. Untruths and exaggerations are not for us.

Let us move from the verbal to the visible:

Distracting mannerisms
Mannerisms, gestures; how important are these? Part of us says, Not at all. We are not joining a school of oratory; we are not aspiring after some esoteric art-form. The studied gesture, the dramatic pause – these things don't sit easily with today's 'cool' television culture.

Besides, Dr. Martyn Lloyd-Jones used to decry the 'professionals', those speakers who were always watching *themselves*.

Do not cultivate or practise gestures. Everything that is histrionic should be avoided.

What is the rule then? It is: be natural; forget yourself; be so absorbed in what you are doing and in the realisation of the presence of God, and in the glory and greatness of the Truth that you are preaching, and the occasion that brings you together, that you are so taken up by all this that you forget yourself completely

(*Preaching and Preachers*, Hodder).

Most speakers would wholeheartedly agree with such advice. We can only be ourselves. And yet I am not content just to leave the matter there. Most speakers have some personal mannerism of which they are largely unaware. If I have a podium in front of me, my right foot tends to wander a little. If left to itself, it ends up twisted around my left ankle. Certainly these little idiosyncrasies need be of no great account. Indeed, when there is no podium, my right foot behaves!

It is when a speaker has developed a mannerism that actually distracts the listeners' attention, that some gentle correction may be called for. I think of one speaker, with whom I rarely feel at *rest*. It is because he delivers most of his address with the weight on one foot only. Consequently he stands at a slight angle, reminiscent of the leaning Tower of Pisa. It is easier *not* to look at him, to receive the full benefit of his message.

Things that Blunt the Talk

With another I can think of, the feet are in ceaseless motion, half a step forward, a step to the side, now a step the other way; you can get mesmerised by those dancing *feet*!

And what does your head do? Some speakers are noted for a forward and down jerk as they make their emphasis; this can come across as provocactive or belligerent

It's the *hands* that come in for the greatest attention! Many speakers are quite unaware of what their hands are doing, and Dr. Lloyd-Jones's advice is probably best – let them be. Most of us have witnessed preaching windmills, the nonstop 'hand-shake', waving the train off and halting the traffic!

I only say to speaking colleagues, Look at yourself on video from time to time; that way you can iron out any mannerisms that seem to get in the way of people receiving the message.

The verbal, the visible; last of all, the *personal*. In what way may *we* blunt the talk?

A stale presence

Here we come to the speaker's *persona*. Before, during and after the talk, what general impression are we conveying? By attitude, appearance, even by our *breath*? They knew all about this in 1875:

'Sankey,' said Moody at dinner in an English hotel one night as Sankey was about to start on his favourite dish of steak and fried onions, 'Sankey, do you expect to speak to anxious souls tonight?'

'Why, yes.'

'Then put down those onions!'

A pause. 'Well! I like my onions, but I like to lead souls to Jesus, so I guess the onions will have to go' (*Moody without Sankey*, J. C. Pollock, Christian Focus).

This applies to alcohol as well. Whether you are teetotal or not, every speaker should keep right off alcohol in advance of the talk. It is not only a question of the breath as the meeting ends and personal exchanges take place. It is that alcohol, by its nature, will take the edge off the delivery. Question times at the close will be adversely affected.

If the meeting is preceded by refreshments, a banquet or toasts, your guard should be up. Stick to orange juice.

I discussed this point once with a university lecturer.

'I follow this policy in regard to my academic lectures,' he told me. 'No alcohol before speaking. As a matter of fact,' he continued, 'it isn't enough simply to abstain on the day. The effect of alcohol can continue for a full forty-eight hours.'

Keep in training, is our axiom. Late nights, sketchy preparation, skimped prayer time will all combine to bring a speaker into the public arena, stale and unready. Vijay Menon's advice for the Christian worker applies to us all: 'Spend time *with* Christ before you spend time *for him*.'

Do the clothes matter? Yes, they do. It seems desirable to dress for a talk in a way that does not display contempt for your audience. The guideline is, dress up, rather than down, if you are the invited speaker. I try, too, to dress appropriately for my own age-bracket. No T-shirts for me, and no trainers or jeans. I cannot claim spirituality

Things that Blunt the Talk

as my sole motive in this respect. It would not be pleasant to be dismissed by my audience as a fading swinger!

*****

Besides, Tommy, there is very great need of preaching now. For iniquity aboundeth, the love of many grows cold, and God's judgements are out in the earth. Tommy, let us preach four times a day, or thirty times a week, whichever you please or can bear better. It will be little enough. Our Master well deserves it ....

Letter from William Grimshaw to Thomas Lee,
July 21st, 1757.
Grimshaw of Haworth, George G. Cragg,
Canterbury Press.

14

HOW TO REACH YOUR CEILING BY 25

The telephone buzzed. On picking up the receiver I learned that Billy Graham was in town and was hoping to come to our Sunday evening service. This kind of thing sometimes happens at churches in the centre of a capital city. I debated with myself; should I or should I not warn our lay reader who was preaching that night? Better warn him, I decided. I looked up David Turner's number.

'David?'

'Hello, Richard!'

'David, it's rather looking as though Billy Graham may be coming to the evening service – it won't make any difference, of course, but I thought I would just let you know.'

I heard a groan at the other end. 'That's all I needed! You'll be there, John Stott, and now Billy Graham! and look at my subject – *Singleness*!'

I had to admit, we might have thought of a slightly more uplifting theme for a travelling grandfather-preacher than the stark 'Now concerning the unmarried....' But not a bit of it. The celebrated evangelist sat riveted to his seat, urging Ruth, his wife, to take notes. Two days later a phone message came through, asking for the cassette recording of the sermon. Three weeks later a letter arrived from his secretary in America, informing us that Billy had been preaching 're-treads' of the lay reader's sermon on singleness, in some youth meetings – and had we, please, any *more* recorded messages in 'the preaching series on Singleness'?

The church prayer gathering loved it, when I narrated the story – but we were profoundly impressed. Here was one of the most effective speakers the world had even seen, at the very height of his powers, and yet humble enough *and hungry enough* to go on learning, whenever the chance presented itself.

Billy Graham, then, gives us our cue when, with perhaps a lifetime of speaking ahead, the question is raised, *How do I keep growing as a public speaker*? The answer is obvious.

Keep hungry

Look out for the story, *William Grimshaw of Haworth,* by Faith Cook (Banner of Truth). Grimshaw, vicar of Haworth during the evangelical revival of the mid-eighteenth century, felt the clouds of guilt and despondency lift off him in 1742, two years after his wife's death. The Bible became a new book to him.

To Joseph Williams, a clothier who knew Grimshaw, it was as though God had 'drawn up his Bible to Heaven, and sent him down another!' Grimshaw's life became lit up by the Scriptures. His congregation grew from twelve to over a thousand. His preaching was described as 'lively'. In what he called his 'lazy' week, he would preach

Keep listening

However there are also numbers of promising speakers who never seem to fulfil their early potential. They seemed so bright, so ready to learn, when they began. But even by their mid-twenties they had apparently reached a plateau. They progressed no further. They had somehow become stuck in a rut. The very aptitudes they had previously displayed for opening the truth to others appeared to have shrivelled.

There must be a number of reasons why this should happen. I suggest that one may be a *gravitational change*. It is possible to become doctrinally hijacked – perhaps by a campus theological faculty that undermines the supreme authority of Scripture. Once you lose confidence in the innate power of God's revelation to change people and situations, you will no longer *listen* to it in quite the same way. Your centre of gravity – as a person of the Book – will have given way, however imperceptibly, to some other emphasis. The edge will have been taken off your desire to get up and proclaim the infallible and inspired Word. It will become something of a chore, and unknowingly you will have ceased to grow.

A loss of speaking momentum is sometimes triggered by *a moral change*. To compromise in matters of sexual purity, for example, is to have stopped listening to the Scriptures and to be disobeying God. An unresolved quarrel with a colleague in the fellowship is enough to block us into a cul-de-sac of our own making, where the Word is not touching us.

Very simply, *a devotional change* can kill the progress of a speaker. It is up to us to 'fan into flame the gift of God' (2 Tim. 1:6), to maintain the daily spiritual glow through the disciplines of Christian living. Nothing can ever replace prayer and the walk with God that should characterise every day. It is a temptation for a speaker to rely upon the *preparation*; to assume that once the material is mastered and the notes completed, that the talk is 'in the can'. Nothing remains but to trot out the prepared words!

It is a fallacy. There lies the way of the detached professional. Eventually the listeners will notice that the speaker's talks are not what they used to be. They may not know the reason, *but it is still noticeable*.

The secret then is to keep listening; listening to one's trusted elders and advisors, listening to one's contemporaries in the fellowship, and listening supremely to God. This last is not a passive exercise, involving the emptying of the mind; it is a conscious application of the mind and will to 'the holy Scriptures, which are able to make you wise for salvation through faith in Christ Jesus' (2 Tim. 3:15). If you think that listening to God is something essentially different from that, it won't be long before you are telling your hearers the same thing in your speaking. The concern will then arise, *Whatever has happened to the talks? They seem to have lost their Scriptural focus.*

Keep humble

D.L. Moody was once asked to introduce Henry Ward Beecher at a meeting. 'Introduce Beecher?' he exclaimed. 'Not I! Ask me to black his boots, and I'll do it gladly!'

True Christian humility is nothing less than living close to the Cross. At the Cross, self promotion becomes archival and looks ridiculous.

The apostle Paul could have been addressing public speakers of every generation when he wrote these words:

> Do nothing out of selfish ambition or vain conceit, but in humility consider others better than yourselves. Each of you should look not only to your own interests, but also to the interests of others
>
> (Phil. 2:3, 4).

If we cannot live this way, we cannot grow; a brittleness, a *hardness* will set in, and we shall be no better than a large, inflated fish in a small pond. Here are four guidelines, designed to keep that sinful ego *down*.

Don't on the stage of your own personality
If you do so, it will become obvious in a score of different ways – not perhaps to the majority of those around you, but to a quiet discerning minority. In conversation, at table, in committee and on the platform, it will become painfully evident that the arrows of your interest, instead of pointing away from you and towards others, are still being directed towards yourself. It can be done with great subtlety, and with a show of spirituality; we may even deceive ourselves in this matter, but if the finger of truth were put on us, the verdict would be that we were thinking of ourselves more highly than we ought (Rom. 12:3).

Don't stint in your praise of other speakers
Again, it is possible to deceive ourselves. We may find it easy enough to praise those who are senior to us in position and experience. It is perfectly possible, too, to congratulate younger up-and-coming speakers and to encourage them – without a twinge of jealousy.

The test is whether we can find it in our hearts to give public acclaim to those who are our exact contemporaries, to set *them* forward, to promote *their* speaking career, to suggest *their* names. That is the test.

There is a wonderful secret with which we must encourage each other. If it should happen that you hear one or other of your contemporaries speaking with powerful effectiveness, and the temptation of jealousy assails you – take action! *Write them a letter*, telling them how well they did, and that you hope, in your own speaking, to emulate them one day. Learn also to praise them publicly.

Shall I tell you what happens? A miracle of grace occurs. The cold stab of jealousy gives way to a warm glow that will fill your soul. Any ugly competitive spirit disperses like the morning mist. And, into the bargain, you will find that you have gained a good friend.

But here is a third guideline:

Don't strain after the limelight

Come to one of the shortest books in the Bible, John's third letter, of one chapter only. Two members of the church are singled out for special mention, Demetrius and Diotrephes. Demetrius has the approval of the whole church and indeed of Christ's apostle (v.12). It is Diotrephes, evidently a figure of authority, who takes the prize for ambitious grasping. He 'loves to be first', warns John (v.9).

No area of Christ's service is free from the desire to be noticed. Why, even the disciples were seen to be squabbling among themselves as to who should occupy top spot. And this at the Last Supper! Only painfully across the centuries has the lesson sunk in that 'many who are first will be last, and the last first' (Mark 10:31). It was George Beverley Shea, the twentieth century's most well-known Gospel singer, who accepted this truth from the earliest days of his career. When urged by friends to take every opportunity of publicising his gifts, he would say 'I can't do that'. And God blessed him. We speakers should take note of his philosophy, given at the age of eighty:

> 'I suggest to young people, Don't put your hand on the knob to open the door; let God do it. He will!'
>
> *Decision Magazine,* April 1989.

And fourthly?

Don't shirk the advice of your mentors
Of course we need to have mentors whose judgment we trust. We must believe that they want our good, and are on hand, not to tear us down, but to build us up.

When exponents of any discipline ignore the advice that they are given, the likelihood is that they have reached the limit of their development.

Speakers, then, can die at twenty-five. Oh, they may go on delivering addresses or sermons for decades, and give useful service ... but it is a nightmare thought that your speaking, at the age of sixty or seventy, will be no better or worse than addresses you gave at the age of nineteen!

Bishop Alf Stanway of Melbourne was a wonderful speaker. I had known him as one of innumerable missionary 'uncles' in Africa since I was two years old. He prayed for and encouraged our whole family from early days. He once said this:

'If you are young, well, all your life is before you. It's a wonderful thing to be young. When I was young and I had energy, I was in love with life and in love with everything. I thought that twenty was a marvellous age – and it is, when you are twenty.

'Well, when I was forty, I thought that was even a better age! And then I became sixty, and my wife said, "Now don't tell me sixty is the best!" But you know, it is! When I was sixty, I asked God that – I didn't know how much more there might be of life – but if it pleased him, to give me *another* ten years of effective ministry; and if I've still got energy then – I'll ask for another ten.

'The man under who I was converted, when he was seventy, asked for ten more, and when he was eighty he asked for another ten; and at ninety – over ninety – he was still being called by bishops to take retreats for clergy and was acting as a curate. The physical powers may go, but the spiritual powers should not go. Why should they go? More days, more strength!'

Uncle Alf is dead now, but ministries such as his should inspire the younger among us; keep hungry, keep listening, keep humble; *keep growing*.

*****

I learned two or three rules, very needful for those who sail between England and Ireland:
1. Never pay till you set sail;
2. Go not on board till the Captain goes on board;
3. Send not your baggage on board till you go yourself.

John Wesley, Journals, August 2nd, 1758.

15

THE TRAVELLING SPEAKER

'All out, please! And everything out of this van. There is going to be a search!'

The barrel of an AK 47 hovered menacingly near the side window.

Garth Hewitt and I were at the end of our tour, and we were having a hard time at Entebbe Airport.

'O *groan*,' muttered Garth in my ear. 'The plane leaves in fifty minutes!'

But sitting with us in the Combi vehicle was our insurance policy, in the form of a diminutive missionary of uncertain years, Lilian Clarke. She knew the country, knew the language, and seemed to know the parents of half the Ugandan cabinet. She had travelled with us throughout the hectic ten-day tour. There were five of us: John the local driver, Garth the singer, Dave Hofer the sound engineer, myself the speaker – and Lilian; she turned out to be the star of the show. Wherever we went, people would come up to her: 'Oh, Miss Clarke, you taught me in Form B3!' We would put her up on the platform, and with her opening greeting spoken in the local dialect, the cheering would begin.

Lilian Clarke was one of those people who knew their way around. The country was still in a state of acute insecurity, following the war that had removed the dictator Idi Amin from power. We had heard the bombs and gunfire in Kampala at night time, and in the last few days had gone through at least a hundred road blocks. Lilian invariably had the right advice every time we were stopped by Dr. Obote's armed soldiers.

'*Ask him how he slept last night,*' she would murmur, and I always complied, Garth meanwhile following up with gifts of postcards of the Queen, lollipops and, when the situation was dire, with the offer of one of his own cassette albums.

This was such a dire moment. The van was crammed with amplifying equipment, massive loudspeakers, musical instruments and our own luggage. A detailed search now would ensure a long stay at drama-ridden Entebbe, and the loss of - how much? But I remembered my drill.

'You'd like us to open everything up? Okay, officer! *How did you sleep last night*?'

'Sleep? Oh, fine. But I'm still very tired.'

'We know the feeling,' I replied. 'We've been travelling all over your country as guests of the Church. On a concert tour! This gentleman' - I indicated Garth - 'is a pop singer.'

'Pop singer?'

I felt something hard pressed into my hand.

'That's right. We'd like to give you one of his albums as a goodbye gift. He is,' I said expansively, 'the leading pop singer in the whole of Europe.'

The soldier looked at the album with interest.

'*Have another one,*' said Garth. 'Take it home to the children.'

A pause.

'All right, drive on; have a good journey.'

We were through.

'It wasn't bribery was it?' Garth and I said defensively to the saintly Lilian, when we were safely in the plane.

'*Not a bit,*' she assured us. 'We want to encourage those poor boys; they have such a dull life!'

Whether the journey is long or short, distant or comparatively local, there is a bit more 'needle' in it for the Travelling Speaker. *Somebody has invited you to come.* There is a Lilian Clark 'missionary' element about it. You are crossing boundaries, you are an experienced traveller ... a veteran?

Treat it always as an honour, when you find yourself on the road, in the train or off to the airport for God and his kingdom. Some are marvellous travellers; others like myself regard it as a major achievement to arrive intact, with nothing broken or lost *en route*. The trick is *never to be parted from your notes*. I will keep them actually on my person or, if overseas for a series of addresses, I will have the rest of the notes with me in my hand luggage. Too often I have been handed a printed slip on arrival at the airport, assuring me that *A world-wide search has been set up for your missing case.*

Stranded once at JFK Airport in New York, having missed my connection and lost my bag, I remember standing in bewilderment as demented travellers swirled around me. At least everyone else seems equally to be in trouble in this place, I mused. *And all this for four talks on Titus!*

'I'm doing this for You,' I prayed, as I took my place *in the line* – as the airport staff described it – a queue that wound itself halfway around the terminal. 'If you want me to get to Asheville,' I continued silently, 'could one spare seat be available for me?'

I got the seat – it was in a tiny propeller-driven craft seating fifteen passengers. I was placed against the emergency escape hatch, and then handed a printed notice, informing me that as I had chosen this specific seat, I was to be appointed safety officer for the flight, and that 'in the unlikely event of an emergency descent', I would be expected to get the hatch open and assist my fellow-passengers to escape! *Was I willing to accept this position*, or would I prefer to change my seat with someone else? I gave the steward a competent nod. 'Fine!' I was in charge. Three airports later I was home and dry. I duly spoke on Paul's letter to Titus.

There is more to this business than preparing a talk and arranging some transport, especially if you have an overnight stay. Had you thought of taking a modest present for your hosts, emergency medical supplies against any unforeseen contingencies, and emergency rations for late at night? A radio to keep you up to date with the news, an alarm clock to ensure your punctual arrival for breakfast, even a little soap and a towel – in the case of conference centres? And, for certain parts of the world, a torch for electrical failures, fly spray for mosquitos and some bottled water for safety? It was a business colleague, David Rennie, who confessed to me that once in a Middle East hotel he found himself in desperation brushing his teeth with Coca Cola.

These concerns seem petty and trivial against the towering and eternal issues that we hope to be challenging our listeners with; but believe me, they will not seem absurd at the dead of night in unfamiliar surroundings.

The Travelling Speaker

The experienced campaigner travels well-equipped, and prepared also for endless delays. 'We apologise to our passengers for the delay,' the woman announcer intoned over the P.A. system at one airport; 'the delay was caused by ... *the delay.*'

And spare notes? It's not a bad idea. There will be occasions when we find that, perhaps owing to a poor briefing or a change of plans, the talk we have brought is completely inappropriate. Indeed, the organisers may have *added* an extra talk to your schedule and forgotten to tell you. Learn to take these things in your stride and not to create a furore when you are taken by surprise. It was a minister friend of mine, Steve Wookey, who liked to recount the visit that his senior colleague once made to a Sunday night service. Though an experienced speaker, he had forgotten that he was supposed to address the youth meeting after the service. He was met at the door.

'Great to see you! All right for tonight?'

'Yes, yes, it's wonderful to be here.'

'And then, of course, there's the youth meeting that you'll be speaking at afterwards.'

Not a flicker.

'You're *right*. And what is my subject?'

'It's Christian Vocation.'

A beam of affirmation.

'*Exactly*! And now if you don't mind, I think I'll just disappear into your washroom for a few minutes.'

At some point the event comes to an end, and you are about to take your leave. Someone comes up to you wearing specs, and holding a pen and pad. 'Could you tell me if you had any expenses?'

In general it's right to put in a claim, if for no other reason than that the organisers ought to know what the actual costs of their meeting came to. They make an annual budget. They need to know, and so do their successors.

Accept whatever you are given. At times I have been paid with book tokens. You wonder, as you drive away, what the reaction would be at the petrol station, if you leant out of the car window and chirped, 'Do you take book tokens here?' But it is all part of the fascinating experience of service, and we learn to take the rough and the smooth together, with equanimity, 'not greedy for money, but eager to serve' (1 Peter 5:2).

This attitude should govern us all, including those who depend on their speaking for a living. Speakers who become money-conscious should either reform their priorities or leave off speaking. The people who *ought* to be giving attention to the question of expenses, fees and salaries are the organising *elders*. They are the leaders responsible for these matters, and they should, if possible, have business people among them. It is not the concern of the speakers. Never.

Were they glad to have you, as a travelling speaker? Were you good company for the family? Did you take notice of the youngest and play trains with them? And how did you leave your bedroom?

It was a hotel chambermaid who told me, 'Down at the meetings, I hear all the comments: *That was a great talk this morning ... I loved Dr. So-and-so this afternoon.* But as for me,' she declared, 'I judge these speakers not by their speeches, but by their bedrooms!'

The travelling speaker.... 'The world is my parish,' declared John Wesley. Certainly he was the world's most travelled individual of the entire eighteenth century. We can hardly emulate *him*. Nevertheless, like him, it is to a dying world that we must address ourselves, in the giving of our lives to this greatest of all privileges. *We are speakers* – and speaking, not, as in Demosthenes' case, for a limited and very temporal cause, but as part of a great line that stretches back to such inspirers of the world as Bunyan and Whitefield, Moody and the Maréchale.

Around the beginning of a new Millennium it is doubly exciting, as we see some of the most effective speakers in the world emerging from such diverse places as Korea, South America, Romania and beloved Africa.

Be part of it. For Christ's mission is criss-crossing the world in every direction. No longer is it from Europe and America to the rest of the world. It is still that to some extent – but the currents are flowing all ways now. And each generation of speakers has enriched the next. I borrow from Spurgeon, from Campbell Morgan, from Carson, Stott and Billy!

I don't feel too bad about that either, because – as my old vicar, Herbert Cragg, used to say, when I was a pale thin young curate almost a lifetime ago – 'Nothing is copyright, as long as it's copied *right*.'

*****

Christian Focus Publications

publishes books for all ages

Our mission statement –

STAYING FAITHFUL

In dependence upon God we seek to help make His infallible Word, the Bible, relevant. Our aim is to ensure that the Lord Jesus Christ is presented as the only hope to obtain forgiveness of sin, live a useful life and look forward to heaven with Him.

REACHING OUT

Christ's last command requires us to reach out to our world with His gospel. We seek to help fulfill that by publishing books that point people towards Jesus and help them develop a Christ-like maturity. We aim to equip all levels of readers for life, work, ministry and mission.

Books in our adult range are published in three imprints.

Christian Focus contains popular works including biographies, commentaries, basic doctrine and Christian living. Our children's books are also published in this imprint.

Mentor focuses on books written at a level suitable for Bible College and seminary students, pastors, and other serious readers. The imprint includes commentaries, doctrinal studies, examination of current issues and church history.

Christian Heritage contains classic writings from the past.

Christian Focus Publications, Ltd
Geanies House, Fearn,
Ross-shire, IV20 1TW, Scotland, United Kingdom
info@christianfocus.com
www.christianfocus.com